The Leader's Edge

The Leader's Edge

THE SEVEN KEYS TO LEADERSHIP IN A TURBULENT WORLD

BURT NANUS

CB

CONTEMPORARY
BOOKS

CHICAGO · NEW YORK

Library of Congress Cataloging-in-Publication Data

Nanus, Burt.
    The leader's edge / Burt Nanus.
        p.   cm.
    Includes index.
    ISBN 0-8092-4420-9
    1. Leadership.   I. Title.
  HD57.7.N36   1989
    658.4'092—dc20   89-32769
                        CIP

Published by Contemporary Books, Inc.
180 North Michigan Avenue, Chicago, Illinois 60601
Manufactured in the United States of America
International Standard Book Number: 0-8092-4420-9

Published simultaneously in Canada by Beaverbooks, Ltd.
195 Allstate Parkway, Valleywood Business Park
Markham, Ontario L3R 4T8 Canada

To Mollie,
Marlene,
and Leora,
my three leaders

CONTENTS

PREFACE ix

1 AMERICA OUT OF FOCUS 1
The Leadership Void 6
Toward a New Perspective on Leadership 7

2 THE CHALLENGE TO LEADERSHIP 11
Prosperity Through Economic Growth 12
Security Through Military Power 16
Happiness Through Self-Realization 17
Failures of Leadership 23
Moving Ahead 28

3 THE NEW AGE 29
Technological Superiority 30
Global Connections 33
Renewal Through Restructuring 37
Lessons for Leaders 40

4 LEADERSHIP MATTERS 45
Understanding Leadership 46
The New Leadership Challenge 52

5 FUTURES-CREATIVE LEADERSHIP 57
Understanding the Future 58
An Extended Model of Leadership 66

6 LEADERSHIP ROLES 71
The Work of the Futures-Creative Leader 73

7 THE SEVEN MEGASKILLS 81
Summing Up 97

8 THE LEADER'S EDGE 99
Taking the High Road 101
Developing Vision 105
Leadership Information Systems 107
Designing Robust Strategies 112
Personal Development 116

9 BUILDING ORGANIZATIONAL CAPITAL 123
Farsightedness: The Future-Oriented
    Organization 124
Mastery of Change: Organizational Capital 129
Organization Design: Building Distinctive
    Competence 133
Anticipatory Learning: The Strategy Process 136
Initiative: Sparking Organizational Innovation 140
Mastery of Interdependence: The Global
    Imperative 142
Organizational Integrity 145
Balanced Growth 147

10 AMERICAN LEADERSHIP
IN THE TWENTY-FIRST CENTURY 149
Farsightedness: National Foresight 153
Mastery of Change: Economic Renewal 159

11 PERESTROIKA AMERICANA 165
Institutional Design: America's Distinctive
    Competence 166

Anticipatory Learning: Educational
   Revitalization   173
Initiative: Entrepreneurship and Innovation   178
Mastery of Interdependence   184
National Integrity   187
Finding Our Way   189

12 EARNING THE RIGHT TO LEAD   191
Who Speaks for the Future?   192
Toward a Renaissance of Leadership   195

APPENDIX   201

NOTES   211

INDEX   217

PREFACE

As THIS IS being written, America has just gone through one of its quadrennial exercises in choosing a new leader. Judging from the pollsters and pundits, many voters were distressed with the choice they were called upon to make. To vast numbers of Americans, neither candidate seemed to offer the qualities of leadership that would be needed to guide the nation in the coming years. Half of the eligible voters were so angered or apathetic that they didn't bother to vote at all. Of those who did, relatively few seemed enthusiastic about their candidate. Even some of the faithful of both parties were heard to say that they wished they had a stronger person to support.

It obviously isn't political leadership alone that bothers people. Managers, investors, and workers complain about poor leadership in business as they watch their companies close down plants and load up with debt. In recent years, American firms have been losing their position as international leaders in one industry after another. Urban leaders seem overwhelmed with problems of crime, housing, waste disposal, air and water pollution, and transportation. Lapses in leadership are everywhere one looks—in education, the media, banking, environmental protection, religion, and even in the home.

It seems odd that this is happening in America, a rich and powerful nation with a proud tradition of leadership spanning more than two centuries. It is even more curious that it should be happening now, at a time of accumulating challenges and threats that would seem to call for the very best qualities of leadership the nation can muster. Stranger still is the sense of helplessness and resignation that too often attends public discussion about leadership.

Americans should react to these developments with a sense of outrage and urgency. The decline of American leadership is not inevitable, not by a long shot. We've had effective leadership many times before, and we can have it again. It is fully within our grasp.

I wrote this book partly because I share that sense of outrage and urgency. I don't pretend to have all the answers, but I have tried to draw upon many sources and my own experiences to demystify leadership. I especially wanted to write about the type of leadership that is becoming necessary to deal with the hectic, complex, and dynamic world we confront as we move into the twenty-first century.

My own interest in leadership has been building for many years. I confess that the subject didn't much interest me as a graduate student in management at MIT in the late fifties. At the time, I was fascinated by computers and their obvious potential to revolutionize management practices. This fascination persisted through my early work at Sperry Rand and the System Development Corporation, and remains to the present day.

A turning point occurred in 1965, however, when I was asked to join the Planning Department at SDC. It was there that I first became aware of the embryonic field of futures research, the systematic study of future possibilities. My interest in the future grew. In 1971, two years after joining the faculty at the University of Southern California's School of Business Administration, I started the Center for Futures Research and served as its director for the next sixteen years.

From the beginning, our work at the Center concentrated on research to understand how the forces for change influence and shape the future. There was a very practical reason for this. If we could understand change, then maybe we could help American organizations figure out how to position themselves to increase their likelihood of growth and survival in a rapidly changing global environment. I called this *normative planning* at the time, to call attention to the study of what organizations *should* do in the future, what their mission *should* be, in contrast to strategic planning that was more concerned with options and alternatives for achieving the mission.

Apart from a little government and foundation support, most of the funding for the Center for Futures Research came from corporate planning departments. I slowly came to realize that these staff departments were not having much success influencing the missions of their organizations.

Another turning point came one day in 1981. One of my distinguished colleagues, Dr. Warren Bennis, shared some of his research findings with me. He had interviewed some successful leaders in depth and tried to distill their views of the leadership function. All of them talked about the pivotal need for vision in leadership. At that point I realized that most of the work we had been doing at the Center for Futures Research would be of much more use to leaders than to their strategic planners. In the next few years, Bennis and I collaborated on a book on this subject called *Leaders: The Strategies for Taking Charge*, which found a receptive audience when it appeared in 1985.

Even as I was working on that book, however, I realized that it did not, and at that point could not, tell the whole story. Something was happening to leadership in America, and nobody seemed to know what it was. To find out, I talked formally and informally to leaders at meetings with executive groups throughout the country. I had more than a hundred leaders fill out questionnaires. My students interviewed another hundred leaders in depth. I went back over the work of the Center and reviewed the writings of others who also were trying to figure out where the country is headed and what it might mean for the art of leadership.

Finally, I sat down to write this book. I do not view it as a final statement, but rather as a progress report on the effects of change on the leadership function in the United States. Since this was to be a broad-ranging inquiry, it was necessary at the outset to make some choices about which areas to emphasize in order to keep the project to a manageable size. Three of these choices were particularly important in shaping the discussion:

1. This book is specifically about the contributions that leadership can make to the success of organizations and the nation. Obviously, factors other than leadership will also play an important role but can't be explored here without greatly expanding the work and losing focus. For example, for organizations to succeed they need, in addition to leadership, resources and technology, skillful management, adequate capital, and educated workers.

2. This book will emphasize the visionary part of leadership, that part most concerned with positioning an organization or the nation in a rapidly changing competitive environment. There are literally thousands of books on the relationship between leaders and followers, and much is known about how to organize, develop, and motivate people. Similarly, many have commented on the qualities commonly observed in leaders such as intelligence, high energy, and determination, and there is a lively debate about whether some of these qualities (e.g., charisma, extroversion) are actually needed. Much less has been written on how the leader knows what is the right thing to do when the outside world won't stand still

long enough to provide a clear picture of what is happening or where it is headed.

3. This book discusses leadership in organizations both large and small, and in both the private and the public sector. However, the most attention will be given to big organizations, since they have the greatest impact on national direction and seem most in need of a new approach to leadership.

By no means do I wish to imply that these other areas are unimportant, or even less important, than the subject of this book. Quite the contrary. However, they have been much explored elsewhere and can be better understood and appropriately applied only if we have a clearer understanding of the meaning and contribution of leadership itself.

Two additional notes of caution: First, although leaders exist at all levels of organizations, examples in this book are usually drawn from those at the very top because they are most easily recognized and often illustrate the intended point most directly. Nearly always, the same lessons can and should apply to leaders at lower levels as well. Second, although there are many outstanding female leaders in this country, including quite a few queried during the preparation of this book, it seems awkward to have to say "he or she" each time one refers generically to a leader. Clearly, no gender slight is intended or should be inferred whenever, for ease of reading, I refer to the leader as "he."

I could not conclude these remarks without acknowledging those who were most influential in shaping my thoughts about this subject. I have already mentioned Warren Bennis, whose work in leadership informed and guided many of my own views in this field. His warmth, friendship, and collegiality have been a constant source of inspiration. For many years Selwyn Enzer, the brilliant associate director of the Center for Futures Research, has been teaching me (and many others) how to think about the future. His meticulous scrutiny and criticism of an early version of this manuscript stimulated new insights which, as usual, proved indispensable to my deliberations. Harry Bernhard, Arthur Schramm, and Stephen Haberfeld also reviewed early drafts and generously offered their sage advice. Robert B. Tucker provided many powerful editorial suggestions on how the presentation could be strengthened.

I owe a great debt of gratitude to these and other friends and colleagues, to the leaders who spoke with me, to my students who taught me, and to the dozens of scholars, too numerous to mention, whose important intellectual contributions also shaped my thinking on this subject. There are echoes of their ideas on every page.

1

AMERICA OUT OF FOCUS

"I look forward to a great future for America, a future in which our country will match its military strength with moral restraint . . . an America that will not be afraid of grace and beauty . . . and a world which will be safe not only for democracy and diversity, but also for personal distinction."

— John F. Kennedy

I ONCE ASKED a colleague whether he was optimistic or pessimistic about the future of America. "Both," he replied. "How can that be?" I asked. "Well," he said, "I have always been an optimistic soul and, after all, things have usually worked out well for this country." "But then why are you pessimistic?" I persisted. "Because," he replied, "there seems to be so little basis for my optimism!"

I was reminded of this little exchange while thinking of the current situation. Surely plenty of reasons for optimism exist. Americans are generally healthy, affluent, educated, and much emulated around the world. The nation is at peace, and unemployment is low. Technological breakthroughs promise a continuing deluge of new products to make life more comfortable, convenient, and carefree.

On the surface, then, there should be only hope and optimism in America today. Instead, the very opposite is the case. Doom-and-gloom articles fill the pages of daily newspapers and provide grist for countless radio and television talk shows. Consider a few headlines in the *New York Times* on a single quite ordinary day—say, Thursday, June 9, 1988:

- U.S. Economic Warfare Brings Disaster to Panama
- Greenspan Sees Harm If Dollar Falls Further
- Senate Upholds Veto: New Trade Bill Is Sought
- AIDS and Money Found to Worry Teen-Agers
- House Passes Bill Limiting Commercials in Children's TV
- Stealth Bomber Is Said to Exceed the Pentagon Cost Estimate by $10 Billion
- Monsanto to Pay $1.5 Million in a Poisoning Case
- House Rejects Home Health Care Bill
- New York Will Rebuild Williamsburg Bridge for $350 Million (bridge condemned to demolition as unsafe)
- Books of the Times: *Merchants of Death, The American Tobacco Industry,* by Larry C. White
- U.S. Agency Cuts Aid to New York Public Library
- Personal Health: The Billion Dollar Price of Quackery

Where's the optimism? If you read further, you'll find a still more sinister message:

- The United States has worked itself into an unprecedented set of financial deficits. Not only are there record trade deficits, budget deficits, and foreign debt, but individual and corporate debt have reached new highs, and the savings rate is among the lowest in the developed world. Add to that the precarious position of the savings and loan industry and the threat of default by some Latin American nations on their debt to American banks, and the financial prognosis for the country can only be described as grim.

- American firms appear to be losing their global competitiveness—not only to Japanese enterprises but to those of numerous upstart Third World nations.

- U.S. productivity growth, once the envy of the world, has averaged less than 1 percent per year since 1973. Only a precipitous drop in the value of the dollar has given some hope to U.S. manufacturers of being able to compete overseas.

- In 1987, nonoil imports added up to 22.7 percent of all domestic goods consumption in the United States. Meanwhile, huge tracts of real estate and major corporations are gobbled up by foreign firms, the better to compete in the American marketplace.

- On a personal level, stress, anxiety, depression, insomnia, suicide, and other signs of insecurity, tension, and hopelessness have become shockingly commonplace. According to pollster Louis Harris, "fully 90 percent of all adult Americans, a substantial 158 million people, report experiencing high stress, with as many as six in every ten reporting 'great stress' at least once or twice every week." Whatever their other failings, Americans have become expert worriers.

Polls on public expectations reveal a nation uneasy about its future. In a 1986 survey, *USA Today* found that only half the respondents agreed that the United States is a better place to live today than it was twenty-five years ago. Even more revealing, only 37 percent believed it likely that the United States will be a better place to live twenty-five years from now.

What ever happened to American optimism? Where is our confidence in the future? Some would answer that the problems today are too tough to solve. But surely the problems themselves are no more difficult than those faced by earlier generations—fighting the American Revolution, resolving issues of slavery and women's rights, or coping with the Great Depression, for example. Besides, Americans have always taken pride in working together to solve tough problems.

The answers must lie elsewhere. Some say Americans are paying the price for the decline of the work ethic and family values, or for a pervasive preoccupation with self and with materialism. Others argue that it is hard to be optimistic when confronted with the threat of nuclear war, AIDS, cancer-causing air and water pollution, and so forth. Some point to what they perceive to be basic flaws in the American system, such as an inability to plan ahead. Others claim that the resources of the nation are stretched too thin due to overextended military commitments in Europe and Asia. Some blame foreigners for taking unfair advantage of American good intentions. Some simply say we're tired.

Other reasons are offered as well, but sooner or later all such deliberations come down to a question of the adequacy of leadership at every level. Would optimism not prevail if Americans had confidence in their leaders and their institutions? They obviously don't. Over the past two decades, confidence in the leadership of *all* major institutions of society has declined precipitously, as shown in Figure 1.

Is it any surprise that people have so little confidence in corporate leaders when they see one after another retrenching in the face of foreign competition instead of moving forward? Is it any wonder that people experience stress and anxiety when important matters in government go unaddressed for years while leaders appear locked in endless rounds of posturing and buck passing? Is the apparent lack of resolve and commitment itself a sign of leadership "rigor mortis"?

FIGURE 1: CONFIDENCE IN INSTITUTIONS

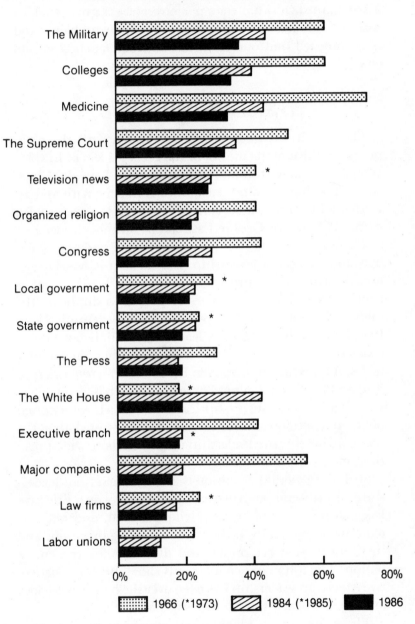

And who's in charge anyway? Americans have become disenchanted by what they perceive to be a great void—a sort of black hole of leadership into which problems and issues are fed and out of which nothing much seems to emerge.

THE LEADERSHIP VOID

The scarcity of leadership today becomes all the more poignant through memories of the great leaders of history. Who today can withstand comparison with Lincoln, Churchill, or Mahatma Gandhi as political leaders; with Martin Luther King or Susan B. Anthony as social leaders; or with Alfred P. Sloan or George Eastman as business leaders?

There are some effective leaders, of course, and occasional outstanding acts of leadership. Lee Iacocca is widely celebrated for turning Chrysler back from the brink of bankruptcy. Steve Jobs appears to be poised to duplicate the great success of Apple Computer in his new venture, Next, Inc. Thousands of effective leaders run small businesses, coach teams, or organize grass-roots efforts in their communities. A few years ago, Warren Bennis and I wrote *Leaders: The Strategies for Taking Charge,* a book based on interviews with ninety successful leaders in which we reported on their common characteristics. We suggested that the *potential* for effective leadership was much more widespread than most people imagine.

Still, the general perception that there are serious leadership gaps throughout American society is correct. Effective leadership is as rare as an Olympic record, and often as temporary, especially at the top of large organizations and institutions that set policy and direction for the entire nation. The following chapter will show just how ineffective American leadership has been over the past two decades and what this dearth of leadership has cost us.

There are plenty of excellent *managers* in organizations—people who meet schedules, control budgets, develop plans, or coordinate the efforts of subordinates to provide a service or product. But *leadership* is another thing entirely.

Leaders take charge, make things happen, dream dreams and then translate them into reality. Leaders attract the voluntary commitment of followers, energize them, and transform organizations into new entities with greater potential for survival, growth, and excellence. Effective leadership empowers an organization to maximize its contribution to the well-being of its members and the larger society of which it is a part. If managers are known for their skill in solving problems, then leaders are known for being masters in designing and building institutions; they are the architects of the organization's future.

Never has the need for leadership been greater. With thousands of our major organizations overmanaged and underled, it is little wonder that anxiety about the future is so widespread in America. The delicate social machinery of government and industry can operate only so long on autopilot. A society or organization without leadership is like the man who fell from the roof of a skyscraper and, as he passed each floor on his way down, was heard to say, "So far, so good!"

Something must be done—and soon—to unleash the potential effectiveness of leaders in America. And much can be done, but only if we first develop a clearer understanding of the character of the leadership that can succeed at this particular time in history and learn how it can be developed and promoted.

TOWARD A NEW PERSPECTIVE ON LEADERSHIP

This is a book about the forces shaping American institutions and what these forces mean for would-be leaders in business and government. Like attendees at a meeting of Alcoholics Anonymous we must start by acknowledging that we are in trouble. Internationally, U.S. leadership is

being challenged in every sphere where American dominance has previously been unquestioned, from economics,
politics, and defense to public health, education, safety, and
even agriculture, high technology, and space exploration.

Such challenges alone would not explain the pervasive
loss of public confidence and trust in the nation's leaders.
However, as will be explained in Chapter 3, this challenge
comes at a time of great transition—a new age—when forces
are coalescing to alter the socioeconomic rules by which
our nation conducts its affairs. During this transition, our
national purpose is blurred. It is less clear what business
America is in, or what business it should be in. The people
sense this ambiguity, and it leaves them doubtful about the
future of their nation and the ability of its leaders to point
the way.

The new age of leadership will not be totally unfamiliar
to many readers, in particular those who read *Leaders*.
Certain characteristics that have served leaders throughout
history, such as the ability to communicate well, to earn the
trust of followers, and to inspire others to action, will still
be important. The major conclusions of our earlier book
will still apply. However, the balance among leadership
characteristics is changing and some, especially those concerned with vision, are taking on much greater importance.

Seven families of competencies—I call them "megaskills"—are needed to exercise effective leadership in the
new age. These megaskills can be learned. A basic assumption of this book is that leaders are not born or made, at
least not by standard educational experiences. Rather, they
create their own leadership potential by developing the
seven megaskills and perfecting their ability to apply them
in real-world, practical situations. Guidelines for learning
them will be provided to help you develop your own leadership skills and to recognize them in others (see Chapters 7
and 8).

The megaskills will be shown to apply equally well to
large and small corporations that aspire to leadership posi-

tions in their industries, as well as to hospitals, universities, public agencies, and other organizations. Some organizations set the tone, pace, and direction for their peer institutions, becoming the models that others seek to follow. In the new age of leadership, the nurturing and deployment of these seven megaskills will mean the difference between those organizations that point the way and those that never quite catch up.

The megaskills will be shown to apply to the entire nation as it seeks new ways to exert international leadership under more challenging circumstances. I will identify actions that America should take and policies we should adopt if we wish to retain a major position of respect, influence, and leadership in global affairs over the next few decades.

Finally, I will show that all of this is interrelated. America cannot exert leadership in the next two decades unless its major organizations can demonstrate leadership competencies and its citizens become successful leaders at every level of society. Much can be done to promote more effective leadership throughout society. Indeed, a great renaissance of American leadership in the next two decades is within reach.

If, as many seem to feel, there is a dangerous and widening gap between leadership performance in America and the requirements of an unstable world, it may be late in the day to call for a new age of leadership. Still, as Ralph Waldo Emerson said, "This time, like all other times, is a very good one, if we but know what to do with it." A good place to start is with a hard look at the new challenges to leadership in America.

2

THE CHALLENGE TO LEADERSHIP

*"To accomplish great things,
we must not only act but dream,
not only plan but also believe."*

—Anatole France

THE BAD NEWS about leadership in America is that it is in deep trouble. The good news is that the bad news need not be a permanent condition. In this chapter, I will review the extent and causes of the leadership void to set the stage for a fresh look at the leadership function itself.

How are we to measure the overall quality of American leadership today? If you were to ask any leader how success should be measured, the response would be predictable—"Just look at what we have accomplished under my leadership." Leaders are totally results-oriented, driven by the need to achieve. So if we want to assess the overall quality of American leadership, the acid test is how successful it has been in achieving the American agenda.

11

Of course, it isn't always easy to know what that agenda is. Americans are a diverse lot; each individual, neighborhood, interest group, and political party has a unique agenda and set of goals. Still, for any society to function at all there must be some basic agreement on what is to be achieved. Even children seem to understand this. A colleague had an athletic ten-year-old daughter who came home from a game one day in tears. She slammed the door and angrily marched up the stairs to her room, muttering, "If there aren't any rules, you can't have any fun!"

For a long time, Americans have had a broad consensus on what they want their society to achieve. The current version of the American agenda has three major elements: prosperity through economic growth, security through military power, and happiness through individual self-realization. Most Americans are convinced that these are attainable goals as long as we are willing to work hard, maintain a free and open society, and have confidence in our own future.

These themes dominate individual conduct, the social agenda, and public expenditures. Above all, they define what we expect of our leaders and provide the measures of their success. By these measures, America was the world champion forty years ago. No other nation even came close to the level of prosperity, security, and individual self-realization then widespread in this country. What is the score now, as the twentieth century races to a close? And more important, are our leaders becoming more or less effective in helping us realize the American agenda?

PROSPERITY THROUGH ECONOMIC GROWTH

Prosperity through economic growth is not just an American preoccupation, of course. Capitalist and communist countries alike define achievement largely in terms of growth in per capita income or gross national product.

FIGURE 2: U.S. PRODUCTIVITY GROWTH

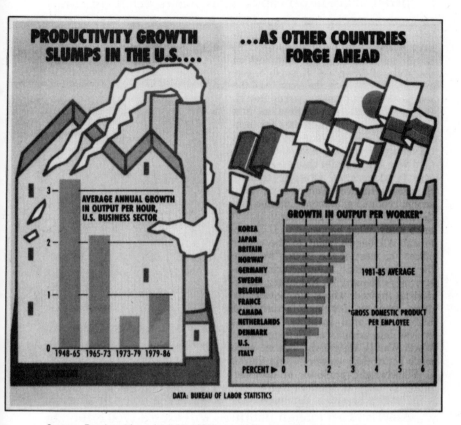

Source: Reprinted from April 20, 1987 issue of *Business Week* by special permission, copyright © 1987 by McGraw-Hill, Inc.

However, nowhere is the pursuit of riches held in higher esteem than in the United States, which owns the world title for conspicuous consumption. Public policy is driven or constrained by the quest for steady economic growth with full employment and low inflation. This is seen to benefit citizens at all income levels, as attested by the oft-quoted aphorism, "The rising tide lifts all boats." Companies measure progress in terms of quarterly or annual growth in per share earnings. When individuals speak about being "well off," it is usually in monetary terms.

America is certainly an affluent society, with a gross

national product exceeding $4.5 trillion. However, U.S. performance in per capita terms, and especially in growth rate, is no longer exceptional. From 1970 to 1985, Canada went from 79 percent of the U.S. per capita gross domestic product to 93 percent; France from 90 percent to 99 percent; Japan from 65 percent to 84 percent; and West Germany from 102 percent to 112 percent.

Behind these trends lie more disturbing developments. Not content with their output and income, American consumers, businesses, and governments actually spent 3.5 percent more than the total GNP in 1987. They didn't spend it on investment. Instead, private consumption was 66 percent of GNP, the highest share since 1950 when World War II veterans were on a family formation binge. The difference was made up with $160 billion from abroad. Most of this was in the form of loans, but foreigners also spent over $40 billion on hard assets like U.S. real estate in 1987. In fact by mid-1988, foreigners had accumulated total U.S. assets worth an estimated $1.5 trillion, nearly one-third more than the value of all the overseas assets held by Americans, and rapidly increasing.

Thus, in the mid-eighties, America switched from being a creditor nation to becoming the largest debtor nation in the world. The International Monetary Fund estimates that America's net foreign liabilities will exceed $700 billion by the end of 1989, or some 15 percent of GNP.

Accompanying this reversal in U.S. credit status, and partly accounting for it, is a lag in productivity growth. In the twenty years prior to 1970, manufacturing productivity in the United States grew at 4.1 percent per year on average. Since then it has grown only about one-third as fast. Though the United States is still highly productive, its productivity is not growing as fast as that of some other nations. In fact, from 1977 to 1987, U.S. productivity went up only 7 percent compared to 23 percent for France, 35 percent for Japan, and 63 percent for Korea. As a result,

American wages have not gone up as much as they might have had the historical growth rate continued.

At the company level, large American firms are fast losing the game they once completely dominated. By mid-1988, there were only five U.S. firms on the list of the world's largest public companies and only one U.S. bank among the world's 30 largest banking concerns.

On an individual level, the Census Bureau reported a 1986 average family income, including social security, of $34,924. This represents substantial purchasing power. Still, on balance, wages and salaries per household, adjusted for inflation, actually *dropped* 8.7 percent from 1973 to 1986, this despite a dramatic increase in the number of two-wage-earner households. Even more significant, most of the growth took place in the wealthiest fifth of families; in the poorest fifth, average family income dropped substantially over this period, accentuating the gap between rich and poor.

For many Americans, making ends meet is becoming much more difficult. Thousands of family farms have gone into bankruptcy. More young people find it a tremendous burden to pay for college or buy a new home. Many older people can't afford retirement or the burgeoning cost of health care. Streets of major cities are filled with more homeless people—some two to three million of them—than at any time since the Great Depression. Millions are unemployed, underemployed, or nonemployable. Public funds for health and social services have not kept up with exploding needs. Millions are still on welfare, many of them children.

So what's the score on prosperity through economic growth during the past four decades? On average, Americans are more affluent than they were. They operate at a higher standard of living, but the prosperity is unevenly distributed both geographically and demographically. For millions of poor people, there is no prosperity at all. Americans are losing ground relative to other nations, having incurred economic debts that will diminish the potential for future prosperity. Many industries are less competitive than they were a decade or two ago. And most striking, for the first time, Americans can no longer take it for granted that each generation is destined to be better off than the previous one.

SECURITY THROUGH MILITARY POWER

Since World War II, Americans have been obsessed with defending themselves against threats of the Soviet Union, its allies, and nations that consider us their enemies, such as Iran and Libya. Since 1945, national defense has consumed a major part of the budget of every administration—some $10 trillion in all. Has the United States purchased security with all this money?

On the positive side, no war has been fought on U.S. soil, and the much-feared nuclear holocaust has not occurred. Apart from wrenching and costly military experiences in Vietnam and Korea, the United States has been at peace during this time. No one doubts that the United States is very powerful.

Security, however, has other dimensions. Peace is not merely the absence of war; it is a sense of safety and freedom from real danger to one's person and property. On these measures, it is not at all clear that, even with its military expenditures of the past four decades, America has achieved a strong sense of security.

Despite huge defense expenditures, the nuclear threat is still very real. Indeed, as more nations acquire nuclear weapons, American vulnerability to misunderstanding, miscalculation, or accident may actually be increasing. The widespread availability of chemical and biological weapons increases this vulnerability.

Terrorism also is a major concern. Our potential for involvement in Central America and the Middle East has not diminished. Concern about the strength and readiness of our so-called conventional forces is widespread.

Even America's control over its own security seems to be eroding. Important military decisions must be shared with allies, many of whom are reluctant to carry their fair share of the burden. Small nations are exacting ever-higher prices for providing military bases. International bodies are less willing to go along with U.S. proposals. Unreliable nations like Iran, Cuba, Syria, and Libya continually challenge America's attempts to maintain international stability. Dictatorships of both the right and left frequently oppose American interests.

Americans are well aware of other sources of danger to life and property than direct military actions. The collapse of the world monetary system, organized crime, and widening drug addiction represent real threats. Environmental threats, such as depletion of the ozone layer, pollution of air and water, and major nuclear plant leaks, could seriously harm the fabric of society. And with the highest rate of violent crime in the developed world, Americans are not even safe in their own homes.

The bottom line is that Americans do not feel more secure. According to one political pollster, "When asked if the world is a safer place now because of Ronald Reagan's defense and foreign policies, a 55%–41% majority is inclined to think that the risk of war is as high as ever." Real security is still a distant dream in America.

HAPPINESS THROUGH SELF-REALIZATION

Happiness through individual self-realization is regarded by Americans as an "inalienable right . . . to life, liberty, and the pursuit of happiness" enshrined in the Declaration of Independence. Freedom, liberty, and equal opportunity are important means to this end. Social security, education, and other benefits help the individual on his or her way.

Americans believe strongly that they should have the freedom to pursue whatever they find rewarding. They feel they owe it to themselves to define and create a successful and meaningful life, to keep growing, to find their own unique sense of significance and self-worth. Some have gone further by becoming so preoccupied with the quest for happiness that all their attention and resources are devoted to a selfish and endless pursuit of personal satisfaction.

There are many domains of self-realization, of course, but three of the most important are work, family and friends, and what is generally called lifestyle. Progress is hard to measure in these areas, but some clues suggest that despite the pursuit of self-realization as a national obsession, we are not doing too well at it.

With regard to the role of work in self-realization, Robert N. Bellah and his colleagues described its several dimensions as follows:

> In the sense of a job, work is a way of making money and making a living. It supports a self defined by economic success, security, and all that money can buy. In the sense of a career, work traces one's progress through life by achievement and advancement in an occupation. It yields a self defined by a broader sort of success, which takes in social standing and prestige, and by a sense of expanding power and competency that renders work itself a source of self-esteem. In the strongest sense of a calling, work constitutes a practical ideal of activity and character that makes a person's work morally inseparable from his or her life. It subsumes the self into a community of disciplined practice and sound judgment whose activity has meaning and value in itself, not just in the output or profit that results from it.

Thus, work plays a much more important role in our lives

than a means to making a living. In a very real sense, it *is* living, one of the distinctive ways people find meaning in their lives. How is America doing in this regard?

In overall employment, the score is reasonably good. Between 1950 and 1990, the labor force will have nearly doubled, largely due to the baby boomers and a female-labor-force participation rate that went from 34 percent to more than 56 percent. More Americans are working today than at any other time in history.

The pattern is not uniform, of course. Considerable un-employment exists in certain parts of the country, espe-cially among blacks and Hispanics. The majority of those who are willing and able to work, even those hard-to-place workers, do have jobs, and that has been true for years. It is also true that many people get a good deal of satisfaction from their jobs, at least according to the national polls. But all is not as rosy as it seems at first glance.

Labor in America is viewed as a factor of production. Economists argue that, as with other factors of produc-tion—like capital and equipment—labor productivity is to be maximized and its cost is to be minimized in the search for a competitive edge. When hard times come, or competi-tion heats up, the quickest way for an employer to cut costs is to pass out the pink slips. Within the past decade, even without hard times, both the frequency and intensity of layoffs have accelerated. A large company that has not had a recent major cutback is a rarity. Foreign competition, a wave of mergers and acquisitions, and the relentless appetite of Wall Street for short-term profits are often blamed.

Downsizing may improve efficiency, but it has high so-cial costs. Those laid off frequently suffer high stress and loss of self-esteem. Professional networks are disrupted. Discharged workers who remain unemployed for long peri-ods experience rejection by scores of potential employers. They may end up in jobs that are less challenging or less remunerative, or even on welfare. The rhythm and structure of family life is disrupted, and the economic fabric of whole communities may unravel. There is no happiness or self-realization for discharged workers.

Even worse than the immediate effects of layoffs are the long-term consequences for society. By making it clear that workers and managers can be terminated at any time through no fault of their own, employers demonstrate that their own loyalties and interests lie elsewhere. Workers reciprocate with diminished loyalty of their own. Why not go across the street for another few dollars per week if there's no security in this job anyway? In fact, economic theory applauds both moves—lowering labor costs and raising labor mobility—as leading to efficiency. The long-term effects, however, may be just the opposite. When firms lose experienced workers, they must pay the high costs of turnover and training; furthermore, they are unable to benefit from the teamwork and know-how built up when people work together for an extended period of time. For the worker, there is a pervasive sense of insecurity and a reluctance to invest too much of himself in a job that may disappear at any time.

General Motors provides a good example of lack of concern for workers. At one time, GM was a model of good industrial relations. Due to uninspired design, poor quality, and a complacent management, its share of the domestic car market dropped almost 50 percent from 1981 to 1987, with earnings plummeting as well. The result? Widespread layoffs. GM's remaining 350,000 production workers received nothing under their profit-sharing agreement except the expectation of even larger layoffs that could affect as many as one-third of them over the next five years. Meantime, the top 850 GM executives split up a bonus pot of more than $350 million in 1987. It should not surprise anyone if GM's workers are consumed with fear, insecurity, and resentment instead of challenge, satisfaction, and self-fulfillment.

Other problems also affect the work world. First, it frequently takes two incomes to buy what one did twenty years ago. Second, some jobs are boring, repetitive, or unsafe, and many people are underemployed, using only a fraction of their skills and talents. Third, according to the Conference Board, as much as one-third of the labor force are part-time or contingent workers. Finally, grossly distorted pay scales allow, for example, executives, athletes, and rock stars to receive massive salaries while teachers, nurses, and police officers must moonlight to make ends meet. These sources of dissatisfaction have increased over the past two decades.

The second area in which Americans seek happiness through self-realization is in their personal relationships, especially with family and friends. It is not easy to tell whether people are happier today in their relationships than they were several decades ago. The traditional family of the fifties is now a rarity. In its place are a variety of living arrangements, many of them temporary. The number of nonrelated people living together has increased 41 percent since 1970. Twenty-five years ago about 39 percent of marriages ended in divorce, while now about 50 percent do. According to a *USA Today* poll, divorced people are only half as likely as married or single people to be happy with their jobs and financial status.

Though Americans still value family life, a variety of additional sources of stress pose threats. For example, because families face the pressure of high costs for housing, medical care, education, and other expenses that often make it necessary for both parents to work, children get less attention. Incidents of child abuse, gang membership, drug use, teen pregnancy, suicide, and other signs of cynical and angry young people are on the rise.

Finally, Americans seek happiness in their lifestyles. Certainly the diversity and freedom of lifestyles available in the United States exceed those of most other countries, where tradition counts a great deal more. However, satisfying lifestyles require spare time. Since 1973, the amount of leisure time available to the average American has actually decreased by 32 percent as more time is devoted to work. Busy Americans also find other satisfactions in short supply—real intimacy, stability, recognition, the ability to make a difference.

Much has been said about the "Me Generation," which is characterized by widespread self-indulgence and preoccupation with appearance, food, health, clothing, and vacations. Perhaps these are compensations for satisfactions not received elsewhere or self-rewards for withstanding the pressures of modern life. There is some evidence that as many as 60 percent of the adults in America feel powerless and alienated—twice as many as twenty years ago—and that one-third of the American people don't lead happy lives.

Of necessity, this review has been very brief, but it should be clear by now that the American agenda is not being realized in important respects. Serious and growing deficiencies abound in all three areas—prosperity, security, and happiness—despite the large amount of attention, resources, and human energy devoted to them. The engine of progress seems to be sputtering.

Why is this so? Surely our skills, talents, energy, and devotion to the American agenda have not diminished. We have more resources than ever to apply to these pursuits. We have much more information and far better tools of organization and communication. Our knowledge base is so much greater. Yet, we seem to have lost our way. Woody Allen once imagined starting a commencement address on this theme with the following words:

> More than any other time in history, mankind faces a crossroads. One path leads to despair and utter hopelessness, the other to total extinction. Let us pray we have the wisdom to choose correctly.

There's no cause for that much doom and gloom. After all, America is the strongest, richest, and most powerful nation on earth. It is a nation full of promise and good intentions, a nation in which hundreds of thousands of immigrants each year invest their dreams and their lives. Still, if the evidence presented earlier in this chapter carries any message at all, it is that we seem to be going off track. A big part of the blame must be attributed to failures of leadership, for it is the leader's responsibility, above all, to always keep us on track by pointing the way to a better tomorrow.

FAILURES OF LEADERSHIP

"People are Yearning for a Leader, but Expecting Much Less," read a *New York Times* headline two days before the 1988 presidential election. Who can blame them? Ample evidence indicates that our leaders are letting us down, and the following sections will focus on three of the most obvious signs of such lapses.

Confusion About Who's in Charge and What Should Be Expected of Them

In 1984, I met with the governors of all fifty states at the National Governors Conference. I was invited to chair a discussion session entitled "Managing Change in State Government." The governors wanted to explore their views on change and the future in a closed-door session, away from their staffs and the glare of the public media. After I told them briefly what we had learned in our research about managing change, they engaged in a lively interchange on how they viewed their responsibilities for change and the roles they wanted to play in public life.

At least two distinct schools of thought emerged about the nature of leadership, at least at the state level. One group thought the job of the leader in a democratic society is to listen to the people and give them what they want. In their view, the people define the issues and express their needs through public discourse, responses to poll takers, and, finally, in the ballot box. The governor's job, then, is to see that the public gets what it wants. According to this group, leadership is a form of followership, with the elected official following the expressed will of the electorate.

The second group of governors took the opposite approach. To them, the leader's responsibility is to help frame the issues in the first place. In this view, the governor helps shape public opinion about what problems the state will face in the future. It is the governor's responsibility to set the agenda and the priorities and to be anticipative, taking preventive action where necessary so that today's problems don't become tomorrow's crises.

Each view drew on valid historical and philosophical precedents. Later I discovered that these were not the only disagreements about leadership in government. For example, I encountered heads of gigantic government departments who swore their only responsibilities were for the implementation of policy made by someone else—a legislature or elected official—even though they issued hundreds of rulings and interpretations that were far more influential in shaping the future of the country than the original directives.

Some high officials in government seem to have little interest in leadership, and see their function as strictly managerial or technical. On the other hand, heads of local offices in some of the same bureaucracies definitely view themselves as leaders.

Nor is there clarity regarding corporate leadership. Some high-level executives told me they thought leadership meant being the boss, giving orders, and enforcing them. In their view, leadership rested with authority at the top, with no room for leadership at lower levels, except to the extent necessary to get workers to carry out the boss's orders. This is far from the concepts of leadership promoted in many firms and taught in major business schools.

Other business executives wondered whether leadership had any role at all in a world where more depended on teamwork and personal commitment than on the exercise of authority. They would put more emphasis on group decision making and consensus management than leadership.

Only military leaders seemed definitive about what leadership is, though some had been distressed to learn through personal experience that the military model doesn't necessarily work in other types of organizations.

In addition to confusion about what leadership is, real leadership gaps exist in important areas. Often there are identifiable leaders associated with only parts of a problem. In the economic realm, for example, the chairman of the Federal Reserve System leads the fight against recession and inflation, but who leads the fight against homelessness, poverty, or underemployment?

Business leaders say that international competitiveness is essential in their industries, yet praise each other for successfully retrenching or going out of business when the competition gets really tough. Who, then, is responsible for ensuring that we don't lose whole industries to foreign competition?

The secretary of defense is charged with anticipating and preparing for military threats, but who anticipates and prepares for threats to security much closer to home—rampant drug addiction or the growth of juvenile gangs?

Confusion about what leadership is and who's in charge, coupled with the complete absence of leadership in some important areas of society, drains energy from organizations, fosters conflict and discontent, and undermines efforts to improve performance.

Failure to Recognize Important Trends

A second conspicuous lapse in leadership is manifested by the inability of many leaders to recognize changes that have important implications for their organizations or for the country. At the national level, for example, the United States no longer has the power unilaterally to shape world political or economic agendas to its own liking, to guarantee foreign borders or international terms of trade, or to prevent the export of good technical jobs. Instead, our nation must consult other strong-voiced nations and transnational agencies; many more matters require multinational negotiations. Still, American leaders resist international collaboration, behave toward the United Nations with barely concealed disdain, and have yet to treat even our closest neighbors, Canada and Mexico, with the respect and cooperation global affairs increasingly require.

In the private sector, the situation is not much better. For example, both Polaroid and Eastman Kodak, the two American photographic giants, failed to recognize the impact that the unfolding electronic revolution would have on camera design. They plodded along for years with only minor variations on their old products. Meanwhile, Japanese competitors captured a large segment of the market by harnessing the potential of electronics to produce 35-mm cameras and video recorders. Similarly, Sears, Roebuck is the world's largest retailer, but it took years of mediocre performance and the loss of millions of customers to specialty retailers and discount stores to jolt them into recognizing that their market had changed and that they'd better do something about it.

Perhaps leaders who failed to recognize important trends that affected their operations always existed. In slower times, it may not have mattered because there was plenty of time to respond, but in the fast-paced modern world, it is far less excusable.

When leaders fail to recognize important trends, organizational adaptability and competitiveness—as well as the entire society—are bound to suffer. Opportunities are lost, often irretrievably. Crash catch-up projects are more costly than measured responses to trends that are recognized early. Investors and employees lose confidence in the leadership; morale suffers; flexibility is diminished; and organizations become defensive. The end result of this failure is

frustration and disappointment as the nation and its institutions fall further and further behind in accomplishing
their purposes.

Ambiguity Regarding Intentions

Whenever I talk to leaders, they invariably say that it is
vital to provide a clear sense of direction. Their subordinates, however, often complain about not knowing where
the organization is headed and how they fit into the larger
picture.

Americans have come to expect ambiguity of intentions
from their government. Political platforms are a hodge-
podge of different agendas, trying to be all things to all
people. In the last presidential election, both candidates
thought they'd get more mileage out of criticizing their
opponent's past record than offering a clear statement of
their own intentions. Contradictions abound, such as when
national leaders advocate balanced budgets while reducing
taxes and increasing spending. At the local level, city
dwellers are often confused about why their elected officials
are trying to attract new businesses to downtown areas
when there are no plans for relieving the traffic congestion
already there.

Confusion of intent is even worse in some corporations.
CSX Corporation, an $8 billion conglomerate, is involved
in so many businesses (e.g., railroads, hotels, fiber optics,
real estate, oil and gas, barges, ocean shipping) that it is not
clear where it sees its future. In General Motors and other
large firms, major decisions on corporate direction often
are compromises made by committees on an ad hoc basis.
With policies of "a little for this division and a little for
that," it is rare for a coherent sense of direction to emerge.

Even if top executives have clear intentions, middle managers frequently complain that they don't know what they
are. Communication is so poor in many firms that each
individual is like a detective, picking up clues about corporate direction from decisions made or from bits of informa-

tion in press releases, newspaper stories, or the rumor mill.

When leaders are unclear about their intentions, or fail to communicate them clearly, people are understandably confused. It is much tougher to coordinate efforts. Actions taken may be contradictory or may even cancel each other out. Under these conditions, progress becomes much more difficult to achieve.

MOVING AHEAD

Confusion about who's in charge, failure to recognize important trends, and ambiguity regarding intentions are not the only failures of leadership that have derailed the pursuit of America's goals. There is also loss of trust, for example, when leaders are found engaging in illegal, unethical, self-serving, or dishonest activities. There is a problem of insufficient attention paid to the development of new leaders and ineffective use of retired ones. There are societal barriers to effective leadership, such as unrealistic expectations and too many constituencies clamoring for attention.

Perhaps, in response to all these problems, Americans have become cynical and resigned, no longer demanding enough from their leaders. Thus there is a massive deficiency in leadership, which has derailed the American agenda. While other factors also figure in the problems of the last decade or two, such as an overly litigious society and skillful foreign competitors, there is no hope of getting back on track without a great resurgence of effective leadership in America at *all* levels of society.

Not just any form of leadership will do the job. We live in a particular time and place, and dynamic forces are at work that will strongly influence the kind of leadership that will work for us. We need to understand these forces and to design a form of leadership that is consistent with them. That is the task to which we next turn our attention.

3

THE NEW AGE

*"It is important to see distant things
as if they were close,
and to take a distanced view of close things."*

—Miyamoto Musashi,
The Book of Five Rings, 1643

ON MY FIRST day in engineering school in 1953, a professor
advised entering freshmen to buy the very best slide rules we
could afford. "After all," he said sagely, "you'll be depending on it all your professional life." I thought of his advice
the other day when I came across my slide rule among some
old papers in the garage. It was in beautiful condition,
having been in its case since the day I graduated in 1957 and
went on to MIT to learn about computers.

Though leadership doesn't change as fast as technology
does, there have been some striking changes since the fifties.
Eisenhower was not the television personality that subsequent presidents have had to be. He governed with a frac-

tion of the staff now associated with the White House. Corporate presidents didn't need to worry much about foreign competition. Many more of them had manufacturing, engineering, or sales backgrounds than the finance, law, or accounting training now common in the executive suite. They knew their businesses from the ground up, and their leadership styles reflected it.

Though the situation has changed dramatically, many leaders have yet to respond fully to the new circumstances. More dramatic changes are likely to occur in the next two decades. These changes are not yet sharply focused, but their broad outlines allow us to glimpse the new type of leadership that will be needed to guide organizations toward survival and prosperity in the future.

This chapter will identify the key characteristics of this new age and spell out some of their implications for leadership. Three factors are particularly important: technological superiority, global connections, and renewal through restructuring.

TECHNOLOGICAL SUPERIORITY

Technological superiority has become one of the preeminent determinants of national and business strength in recent times. Economic productivity and military defense depend on it. Good jobs and access to financial resources are the direct result of remaining at the cutting edge of technology. National vitality and adaptability are related to innovation and entrepreneurship which, in turn, are heavily dependent on technology.

As we look ahead, the rapid technological changes of the last two decades will seem tame compared to the veritable explosion in technology that can be expected in the next two decades. The pace of technological change will continue to speed up as a result of six "accelerator" technologies:

1. *Computers and communications* are now poised for major breakthroughs in artificial intelligence, factory automation, and home delivery of information services.

2. *Genetic engineering* is about to unleash major improvements in medicine, agriculture, and pollution control.

3. *Space sciences* will lead to improved communications, factories in orbit, and untold rewards from space exploration.

4. *Superconductivity* will permit superfast computers, high-efficiency power generation and distribution, and low-cost, high-speed rail transportation.

5. *New materials*, such as specialty polymers, ceramics, composites, and microsponges, will evolve.

6. *Laser and holography techniques*, for applications as diverse as photography, computer memory, medical surgery, and fusion reactors, will unfold.

Any *one* of these technologies would justify expectations of rapid technological growth in the next two decades, but *all six* are on the verge of major breakthroughs. Furthermore, each of them has properties that tend to accelerate all the other sciences and technologies by making it possible to "see" tinier or more distant objects, to handle previously impossible computational challenges, to create new substances and even life forms, or to shed new light on the physical, biological, and chemical mysteries that remain on our planet.

To appreciate the magnitude of the consequences these technological changes have for leadership, consider just one of them—the so-called Information Society. At a minimum, information technologies will change organizational forms, modes of communication, and the decisions that leaders are called upon to make. Millions of ordinary people will have access to a wide range of information services such as teleshopping, electronic mail, remote medical consultation, office automation, interactive education, and library services. Workers will use teleconferencing, and many will telecommute (instead of going to work, work will come to them electronically), at least part-time. Information will increasingly become a global strategic weapon in business.

In an earlier book, we showed how the marriage of computers and telecommunications, resulting in large geographically dispersed information networks, may result not only in substantial cost savings and greater information access, but also in totally new institutional forms:

A large distributed network of computers, software, terminals, and data bases provides an ideal *production facility*. That is, new services can be manufactured through providing added value to existing services; producers can pool resources to achieve economies of scale; suppliers can specialize in processes and products in which they have a competitive edge; and there is even room for a small producer or cottage industry to custom tailor services to an individual user's specifications. The aggregation of interconnected resources provides a massive production facility which enables producers to purchase only what they need of each of the factors of production, and to change the mix easily and quickly as production demands change.

Network services provide access to scarce or infrequently needed resources, which an individual cannot justify owning, and provide rapid mobility of information among and between the community of individuals and institutions who form the network. What is new and important about this *medium of communication* is that it provides extremely rapid transfer of symbols and images at much higher density than human conversation, at much greater speed than the postal system, and with much greater selectivity than television and other mass media.

Network information services link tasks, people, resources, and management into various configurations of both temporary and permanent *organizations* so as to permit coordination and control of dispersed functions. Moreover, multiorganization structures can coexist in the system simultaneously. . . .

All the usual services of a *marketplace* can be offered within a large information network. Products and services can be advertised; buyers and sellers can be located; ordering, billing, and delivery of services can be facilitated; and all manner of transactions can be consummated, including wholesale, retail, brokering, and mass distribution.

This example suggests how just *one* of the accelerator technologies is likely to impact on other technologies, institutions, and processes throughout the economy and society. Each of the six accelerator technologies is at a similar launching point, interacting with all the other sciences and technologies to speed up their development. No product or service, no organization, and no aspect of society can remain the same in the face of such a set of forces.

No nation can be strong without maintaining technological superiority. No leader can earn credibility without giving technological superiority a high priority on the organization's agenda, as leaders will be expected to help their organizations make full use of their technological potential. Leaders must master the art of conducting frequent technological transitions, each of which could radically alter the processes, products, and fundamental structures of their organizations. Those leaders unable to do so will be worse than ineffective; they will become dangerous obstacles to organizational vitality and survival.

GLOBAL CONNECTIONS

For centuries, a nation's progress depended almost entirely on what went on inside its own borders. Progress was derived solely from the natural endowments of the country, the ingenuity and energy of its people, and the wisdom of its leaders and their policies. Although these factors are still crucial, progress now depends more and more on agreements with other nations, forces outside national boundaries, and the actions of organizations and institutions that transcend national boundaries.

The same applies to business. Multinational companies have gained considerable financial strength through economies of production and marketing. They are able to coordinate their global operations with multinational information systems. They can be enormously innovative by taking advantage of pools of specialized talent in many countries, and by nimbly transferring ideas, products, and processes across national boundaries. Many markets are stratified on a global rather than a national basis. Marketing research, advertising, and product development are all geared to international markets in many products and services. Competitive actions on products or pricing are felt immediately all over the world. Production and research are allocated to countries that have a cost or quality advantage, and products often consist of components made in many countries. For example, the 1989 Pontiac Le Mans was designed in West Germany; has fuel, steering, and transmission systems from the United States; sheet metal from Japan; radio from Singapore; and engine, tires, electrical system, and assembly in South Korea.

Thus while cultural differences remain, the world is fast moving toward becoming a single marketplace, a single labor exchange, a single production facility, a single research center, and a single financial entity. No nation, even one as large and powerful as the United States, can go it alone anymore. America cannot even control its own interest rates, the prices of its own raw materials, or the value of its own currency without international consultation and often collaboration.

Global interdependence is most obvious in the defense area, of course, where both the United States and the Soviet Union must consult with allies who have their own agendas and interests. Many defense issues—including regional wars and arms races, terrorism, human rights violations, rogue states, protection of international shipping, transborder drug traffic, illegal immigration, and organized crime—cannot be addressed at all except in international forums.

Similarly, we are locked into global interdependence in a variety of technical and environmental areas. Weather fore-casting, civil aviation, space telecommunications, and joint scientific research in Antarctica all demonstrate the power of international collaboration and integration.

Environmental threats make an even more compelling case (see Figure 3). Chernobyl showed that radioactivity does not respect national borders, and Bhopal showed that technology transfer from one nation to another may carry deadly risks. Acid rain, the depletion of the ozone layer, deforestation and desertification, the extinction of species, hazardous waste disposal, overfishing, oil spills, and many other environmental threats typically involve many nations, and progress can be made only through international col-laboration.

The internationalization of these four areas—economics, defense, technology, and the environment—together with other areas such as transportation, world hunger, illiteracy, and disease, will only become more intense in the next two decades. The world's peoples, institutions, and nations will discover it to be in their own interest to find joint solutions to problems. The European Economic Community is an example of how in a few decades nations can integrate their activities despite centuries of independent development, different languages and cultures, and even a recent history of hostilities.

The most immediate implication for the United States is likely to be rapid progress in integrating its interests with those of its closest neighbors, Canada and Mexico. Beyond

FIGURE 3: THE EARTH'S VITAL SIGNS

Forest Cover Tropical forests shrinking by 11 million hectares per year; 31 million hectares in industrial countries damaged, apparently by air pollution or acid rain

Topsoil on Cropland An estimated 26 billion tons lost annually in excess of new soil formation

Desert Area Some 6 million hectares of new desert formed annually by land mismanagement

Lakes Thousands of lakes in the industrial north now biologically dead; thousands more dying

Fresh Water Underground water tables falling in parts of Africa, China, India, and North America as demand for water rises above aquifer recharge rates

Species Diversity Extinctions of plant and animal species together now estimated at several thousand per year; one-fifth of all species may disappear over the next 20 years

Groundwater Quality Some 50 pesticides contaminate groundwater in 32 American states; some 2,500 U.S. toxic waste sites need cleanup; extent of toxic contamination worldwide unknown

Climate Mean temperature projected to rise between 1.5 and 4.5 degrees Celsius between now and the year 2050

Sea Level Projected to rise between 1.4 meters (4.7 feet) and 2.2 meters (7.1 feet) by the year 2100

Ozone Layer Growing "hole" in the earth's ozone layer over Antarctica each spring suggests start of a gradual global depletion

Source: "The State of the World, an Interview with Lester Brown," *Technology Review*, July 1988, 53. Reprinted with permission from *Technology Review*, © 1988.

that, America may well find itself having to evolve a new geostrategy, as suggested by Zbigniew Brzezinski in a recent issue of *Foreign Affairs*:

> The global economic hierarchy by the year 2010 might be the following: first, the United States (with a GNP just under $8 trillion); second, the European Economic Community (with a similar or perhaps even larger GNP but lacking the attributes of a single political power); third, China (with a GNP of just under $4 trillion); fourth, Japan (with roughly the same GNP); and then only fifth in rank, the Soviet Union (with a GNP of just under $3 trillion).

With greater interdependence among nations, organizations, and people, leaders will be expected to develop worldwide networks so that their organizations can enjoy visibility and new opportunities. With a variety of forces conspiring to bring the world closer together, leaders must learn to be comfortable in diverse national and cultural settings, becoming true global citizens.

RENEWAL THROUGH RESTRUCTURING

American institutions have always been resilient enough to make the myriad small adjustments necessary to cope with change. About ten years ago, however, the American economy, polity, and society began to confront circumstances that call for major restructuring. That process, albeit begun with little conscious direction from Washington and even less recognition by the general public, is under way.

The initial economic stimulus was from the OPEC oil embargo, which ended decades of cheap energy and resulted in large capital transfers from the United States to Arab nations. The Arabs placed their oil wealth in U.S. banks, which promptly loaned it out to Third World nations. These nations, struggling just to meet the interest payments, may never repay the full debt. Thus, even under the best of circumstances, the American banking system will be held hostage to its foreign debt portfolio for years to come.

Other economic problems piled up in the eighties. Large budget deficits accrued, making the interest on the national debt a major element in future federal budgets. Massive import-export imbalances maintained a high level of consumption that turned the United States from a creditor nation to the largest debtor nation in the world. The U.S. banking system groaned under the weight of bad loans on overvalued farm properties and real estate in the oil patch. The economy faced massive deferred costs that will have to be paid in the next two decades, including costs for toxic waste cleanup, road and bridge repair, and the future costs of large defense projects such as MX and "Star Wars." The U.S. economy is clearly out of balance.

To negotiate these economic perils, it is absolutely essential that the United States improve its competitiveness in world markets. Indeed, America will have to export much more than it imports for many years to come to pay the interest and principal on its foreign debts. Yet, over the past two decades, the United States actually has been losing its competitive position in many industries to other countries. As suggested in Figure 4, we now export cheap basic materials and import high-valued manufactured goods, a pattern more characteristic of developing nations than highly developed countries.

Thus far, halfhearted attempts have sought to revitalize some of the affected industries through "voluntary" import constraints, devaluing the dollar, and deregulating the telephone, transportation, and energy industries. Instead of creating more competition, however, managers have used these incentives to diversify out of the affected industries or to seek short-term gains through clever financial manipulations.

FIGURE 4: WEST COAST EXPORTS/IMPORTS

West Coast Containerized Exports Fourth quarter, 1987		West Coast Containerized Imports Fourth quarter, 1987	
Product	**TEUs***	**Product**	**TEUs***
Waste paper	66,000	Wearing apparel	46,000
Logs and raw lumber	33,000	Auto parts	39,000
Cotton	30,000	Furniture	37,000
Animal feed	23,000	Footwear	36,000
Fruit	20,000	Toys	21,000
Resin	17,000	Television equipment	20,000
General cargo	13,000	Computers	15,000
Vegetables	13,000	Tires	14,000
Meats and poultry	12,000	Bicycles	10,000
Wood pulp	9,000	Misc. electrical products	10,000
Hides	8,000	Misc. plastic products	9,000
Aluminum scrap	8,000	Cooking ware, irons, heaters	9,000
Nuts	7,000	Hardware	9,000
Mixed metal scrap	6,000	Misc. machinery	8,000
Cardboard boxes	6,000	Engine motors	8,000
Field seeds	6,000	Radios and stereos	7,000
Lumber boards	5,000	Canned foodstuffs	7,000
Borax	5,000	Beer and ale	7,000
Newsprint	4,000	Motorcycles	7,000
Benzenoid chemicals	4,000	Automobiles	6,000

*A TEU is a "20-foot equivalent unit." A 40-foot container, for example, holds two TEUs.

Source: Los Angeles Times, June 7, 1988, Part IV, 2. Copyright, 1988, *Los Angeles Times*. Reprinted by permission.

This cannot, and very likely won't, continue. Dozens of proposals for restructuring the economic base have already been put forward, including various forms of national planning, investments in new industries, enhanced entrepreneurship, and new worker arrangements. Corporations have already begun to restructure through mergers, more decentralized organizations, emphasis on entrepreneurship, and increased attention to teamwork, quality, and customer service.

Changes are also taking place in political structures. Political power is flowing from the federal government in both directions. Some power is flowing upward to international agencies and treaty organizations, as decisions require multinational support and joint actions. Domestically, political power seems to be flowing downward to states and regions, as local entities take more responsibility for their economic development, transportation and communication infrastructures, and social services.

In short, America is trying to renew itself by striking a new balance through its own political, economic, and social restructuring. This means a constant rearrangement and blurring of organizational boundaries, making it necessary for leaders to have a great tolerance of ambiguity. In addition, leaders will have to become highly skilled as negotiators and designers to create new organizational arrangements, and as spokespersons to explain structural changes to a variety of internal and external constituencies.

LESSONS FOR LEADERS

These three forces—the drive for technological superiority, global interdependence, and pervasive and continuous restructuring—are not the only ones that will shape America in the next two decades. Demographic shifts, changes in values and lifestyles, new political agendas, and the like will profoundly challenge both leaders and their organizations. The effect of these forces will be threefold: to make everything attempted more fluid, more complex and uncertain, and yet more impactive.

More Fluid

As society restructures, stability in structures, processes, or cultures is disturbed. Global integration subjects any organization to shocks from anywhere in the world at any time. With technology feeding upon itself, knowledge has a shorter life span. As Hasan Ozbekhan noted more than twenty years ago:

> Events of this magnitude have a price. The price of this particular event is, in all probability, that sense of strange and powerful disquiet we feel before the heaving horizon that confronts us. Old institutions, known ways of life, established relations, defined functions,

well-traced frontiers of knowledge and feeling move
and change as we go; we are constantly subjected to
new configurations of perceived reality; we are constantly asked to adapt faster and faster to requirements
generated by new information, by a narrowing yet
always moving and always changing physical environment, by an increasingly confused yet proliferating set
of goals, outlooks, and aspirations. It is as though the
entire environment of man—his ecological, social,
political, emotional, and physical space—were becoming less solid, less permanent and less constant. It
looks as if we were in the midst of a vast process of
liquefaction.

As the pace of change accelerates due to these forces,
organizational tempos speed up; lead times are reduced.
Instead of solving problems, the leader is more often called
upon to steer the organization through dynamic and perilous situations. Rapid change makes it difficult to use the
past or even the present as a basis for decision making and
makes it much more critical to understand the forces shaping the future. All of this puts a premium on the leader's
ability to anticipate, monitor, and manage change. As Tom
Peters says in his recent bestseller, *Thriving on Chaos*,
"Today, loving change, tumult, even chaos is a prerequisite
for survival, let alone success."

More Complexity and Uncertainty

Global integration, restructuring, and technological expansion are all being played out in large macrosystems,
gigantic sociotechnical organizations that impact on their
environments at many points and interact with each other
in ever more complex arrangements. Consider, for example,
the international banking system; the United Nations with
all its subsidiary instrumentalities; satellite television networks; the global air transportation system; and even organized crime.

Moreover, this is a time of transition, in which both old systems and emerging new ones may be working side by side for some time. One of the most critical effects of the operation and interaction of global macrosystems is greatly increased interconnectedness and complexity, which threatens man's ability to understand cause-and-effect relationships.

Uncertainty usually accompanies complexity. Global integration increases uncertainty as the number of actors proliferates. Military and economic threats may or may not be carried out; cartels, treaties, and joint ventures may or may not have the intended effects. Technological breakthroughs are inherently uncertain, of course, but even more unsettling may be the unexpected consequences of technological progress, such as its impact on health, the environment, or lifestyles. Restructuring is also inherently unpredictable, as new demands by stakeholders clash with tradition.

One wag suggested that if you're not confused, you're not thinking clearly. Thus another essential requirement of a new type of leadership is a high level of skill in handling complexity and uncertainty.

More Impact

Global integration, technological change, and restructuring conspire to give organizational decisions explosive impact. In an age in which scientists can manipulate genetic material, societies can reconfigure the historic role of women and family, and corporations can rapidly move jobs around the globe, the stakes have gone way up. Decisions made anywhere affect everywhere and have repercussions on millions of people. The responsibility of organizations and leaders for their actions has become truly awesome.

The great increase in impact and risk places a premium on the ability of leaders to cope with stress. Often, commitments must be made on the basis of information the adequacy or relevance of which is doubtful. Indeed, the death of certainty is the birth of leadership, for it is the unique responsibility of the leader to replace perplexity with a meaningful sense of purpose.

Unfortunately, too many leaders today fail to recognize that circumstances have changed and that leadership also must change. They remind me of the opening paragraph in *Winnie-the-Pooh*:

> Here is Edward Bear, coming downstairs now, bump, bump, bump, on the back of his head, behind Christopher Robin. It is, as far as he knows, the only way of coming downstairs, but sometimes he feels that there really is another way, if only he could stop bumping for a moment and think of it. And then he feels perhaps there isn't. . . .

Here and there are examples of leaders who understand that great changes are taking place, who are trying to respond to and even shape them. But this is not enough. America cannot prevail in the nineties unless all of our major institutions have leaders who are attuned to the realities of this frenetic new age. We need to go back to basics, review what we know of leadership, and redefine it for the challenges of the world ahead.

4

LEADERSHIP MATTERS

"The greatest need for leadership is in the dark. . . . It is when the system is changing so rapidly . . . that old prescriptions and old wisdom can only lead to catastrophe, and leadership is necessary to call people to the very strangeness of the new world that is being born."

—Kenneth Boulding, *Human Betterment*

LEADERSHIP IS A peculiar property of the human species. Throughout history, it has been broadly practiced, praised, and pilloried. Countless philosophers, scholars, and poets have consumed oceans of ink and forests of paper on the subject. And yet, at the end of this long trail of insight and introspection, there are few markers for the future and a maze of contradictions to unravel. For example, consider the following:

▷Like other human qualities, such as love and beauty, leadership is extremely important and can be achieved only with considerable effort. But also like love and beauty, there are different paths to successful leadership, and most practitioners are self-taught. There is no simple cookbook on leadership.

▷Most of us can recognize good leadership when we see it and may even experience it personally from time to time. However, when called on to describe it, despite all we have seen, read, and experienced about the subject, we are unable to detail the essence of leadership. It is somewhat like describing virtue—we know that Mother Teresa has it and Adolph Hitler didn't, but the wisest people in history have not been able to agree on exactly what *it* is.

▷Leadership appears to be partly culture-dependent in that standards and expectations of leaders differ among cultures and within the same culture from time to time. An Ayatollah is expected to be more spiritual and less progressive than a French president. An orchestra leader is expected to be more intuitive and aesthetic than the head of a dog food company. The president of Ford Motor Company or Westinghouse must be more of a global citizen than Henry Ford or George Westinghouse had to be.

Thus it is important to consider what leadership qualities are in demand at this particular time in America's history. The question is how to position the country and its institutions for the next two decades. Now is the time to develop a model of leadership that conforms to the realities of the new age.

UNDERSTANDING LEADERSHIP

At the simplest level, leaders are easily recognized as those who take charge, who make things happen in an organizational or societal context. Whenever people are engaged in common enterprises, an opportunity and, indeed, a necessity for leadership arises. But what *is* leadership? In a classic of management literature, Chester I. Barnard defined it as follows:

Leadership . . . is the indispensable social essence that gives common meaning to common purpose, that creates the incentive that makes other incentives effective, that infuses the subjective aspect of countless decisions with consistency in a changing environment, that inspires the personal conviction that produces the vital cohesiveness without which cooperation is impossible.

The literature of leadership follows several well-worn paths. For a long time, the concentration was simply on the deployment of power and authority, as exemplified in Machiavelli's *The Prince.* Then attention shifted to the so-called traits of leadership (e.g., charisma and self-confidence) and styles of leadership (e.g., autocratic or participative). More recently, behavioral scientists have turned their attention to the leadership situation itself—interactions between leaders and followers, the purpose of the group or organization, and the way it works.

A few years ago, Warren Bennis and I took another look at leadership as it actually is practiced. We asked ninety well-known leaders how they saw their job and what strategies they employed. Sixty were chief executive officers of major U.S. corporations, and the rest included government officials, academicians, orchestra leaders, and football coaches. The results, reported in our book entitled *Leaders: The Strategies for Taking Charge,* drew a sharp distinction between what leaders do and what managers and administrators do.

Managers are concerned with doing things right. Deeply involved in the processes of running their organizations, they are responsible for guiding operations so that they are conducted efficiently, at minimum cost, and on schedule.

Leaders care about these things, too, but they concentrate on effectiveness rather than efficiency. They focus on doing the right thing and on choosing what should be done and why, not just how to do it. They are more deeply involved in the overall *direction* of the organization rather than in *process,* making sure that the organization is doing what it should be doing to earn its legitimacy, its future access to resources, and its strength, growth, and long-term survivability.

Managers are largely internally focused, heavily involved in deploying capital, labor, and technology. Much of their attention is devoted to budgets and goals or the challenges and issues that demand immediate attention. Leaders are also interested in the organization, of course, but are externally focused, seeking the appropriate path for the evolution of their organization or social movement. Their interests and impacts tend to transcend organizational boundaries to include many external constituencies. Rather than simply deploying resources, they are vitally interested in structuring the aspirations and expectations of their followers and helping to translate jointly held intentions into reality.

To achieve efficiency, managers seek stability, predictability, and control. Their thinking processes tend to be analytical and convergent, forever seeking solutions to problems and dealing with the inevitable crises and opportunities that arise in any enterprise. On the other hand, leaders are more interested in flexibility and change than in stability and control. Their thinking processes tend to be more intuitive and divergent.

Managers usually work within given structural parameters, while leaders are free to change structures. If managers are primarily problem solvers, leaders are, or should be, primarily institution builders.

Obviously, both leadership and management are necessary in any organization. Although it is rare for an individual to be equally skilled in both areas, in some cases one individual may fill both roles. However, most leaders we interviewed saw leadership as a full-time job and therefore delegated management responsibilities.

At this particular time, it appears that large American institutions, both in business and government, are overmanaged and underled. It is possible to be in full mastery of the ship and still have no sense of direction. Schools of business, public administration, and management, and their counterparts in other fields such as health and education, have done a splendid job of training managers. No one, with the possible exception of the military, has taken responsibility for educating leaders. Like parenting, leadership is learned mostly on the job, and mistakes are very costly. Fortunately, also like parenting, all of us have some leadership talent that can be developed with the proper encouragement and direction.

According to those interviewed for the earlier book, leaders use four strategies for taking charge:

1. Management of attention. Effective leaders have agendas and are very results-oriented. They have a vision—a realistic, credible, attractive image of the future—that they espouse and persuade others to accept as worthwhile and meaningful. Vision is important because it creates focus, becoming a target that beckons, a direction to which people can become committed, and a basis for the establishment of goals and objectives.

2. Management of meaning. People can work together effectively only if they have a shared interpretation of reality. Leaders articulate, define, communicate, and organize meaning to help people understand what is going on. They interpret developments elsewhere in society and help people understand their significance and implications for the organization. They also create organizational cultures or social architectures; that is, leaders institutionalize roles, missions, structures, relationships, and measures of performance that form the context within which managers and workers can carry out their operations. In short, leaders tend to legitimize what they feel is worthwhile to want and to do.

3. Management of trust. Trust is the glue that binds leaders and followers together. Because it can't be mandated or bought, it must be earned, and leaders earn trust by taking positions, making those positions known, and sticking to them. Trust implies reliability, predictability, and mutuality of concern. It depends on integrity, on standing for something honorable and worthwhile even if it involves personal loss.

4. Management of self. Leadership is the healthy and creative deployment of oneself. Leaders know their strengths and weaknesses, their worth and limitations. Because they understand themselves they are able to accept advice without feeling threatened and to treat every mistake or setback as an opportunity for learning. Leaders learn, and they help others learn by setting a good example, rewarding learning when they see it, reinforcing innovation and creativity, and seeking broad participation in the search for new directions. They do not need constant approval themselves but understand the value of expressing appreciation for the contributions of others.

These four strategies of leadership were seen as what make it possible for leaders to translate intentions into reality. Leaders seem to learn early in their careers that what appear to the uninitiated as the strongest parts of an organization—the resource base, buildings and facilities, organization structures—are in truth the most fragile and ephemeral, subject to being blown over or made irrelevant by the slightest shift in the winds of change. Leaders know, or perhaps sense, that the strongest, most durable and substantial parts of an organization are the satisfaction, commitment, and sense of direction shared by members of the organization. These intangibles are the real pillars of the organization, capable of sustaining it even in the worst of times.

Leadership has very little to do with the exercise of raw power although, of course, leaders do possess the authority to take unpopular actions when needed. Rather than using power to direct, control, prod, push, or otherwise manipulate people, however, leaders seem to accomplish more, at least in America, by using positive approaches. Effective leaders empower others by inspiring them, energizing them, and aligning their momentum so that mutually reinforcing activities result. In his Pulitzer Prize–winning book, *Leadership*, James MacGregor Burns said it this way:

> It is the exercise of leadership rather than that of naked power that can have the most comprehensive and lasting causal influence as measured by real change. This is so because leaders engaging with the motivations of followers and of other leaders at all levels of movements and organizations are able to exploit the massed social energies of all the persons consciously involved in a joint effort. There is nothing so power-full, nothing so effective, nothing so causal as common purpose, if that purpose informs all levels of a political system.

Empowerment works because it supports the deepest psychological needs of followers. People want to make a difference, to be where the action is. They want to feel they are doing a good job and want recognition for it. They want to join with others in a community of common purpose, to enjoy their work and not be consumed with what appear to be pointless exercises. The leader who meets these needs has little trouble capturing the commitment and trust of colleagues.

Thus leadership has less to do with using others than with serving them. People are well served when they can feel pride in being part of a useful and successful enterprise. They are well served when able to perform professionally and competently and experience satisfaction in what they do. And they are well served when they reach their true potential as workers, colleagues, and as human beings. In the final analysis, leadership is making people into effective collaborators in the important work of organizations, institutions, and society.

Most thoughtful leaders today probably would agree that the foregoing is a fair depiction of what they are trying to do. It shows the leader as being concerned with relationships to followers (trust, communication, empowerment); to organizations (shared meaning, common purpose, organizational culture); and to the outside world (vision). The description is an eminently reasonable, clear, consistent, and even humane view of leadership. And yet something is not quite right.

THE NEW LEADERSHIP CHALLENGE

How can we reconcile this view of leadership with the disturbing realities of the prior chapters? Americans no longer are as successful as they once were, or want to be, in achieving their dreams of becoming more prosperous, more secure, and happier. What have leaders been doing all this time? Why is there such an enormous chasm between the national need for effective leadership and the undistinguished record of American leaders in the past twenty years or so? Why have they not been leading their organizations and constituencies in the new directions so clearly indicated by the changes taking place?

I don't think the answer is that there is a dearth of leadership talent, that we have overworked or undervalued our leaders, or that large numbers of leaders are incompetent, lazy, or corrupt. In fact, leaders are present at every level of American society. Far from being undervalued, effective leaders are well regarded, some elevated to heroic proportions (such as Lee Iacocca). They certainly are well paid—many will say *too* well paid. By and large, most work very hard, and the few corrupt ones are soon exposed in an open, news-hungry society.

So why aren't American leaders more effective? Part of the answer is that many do not fully put into practice the unmistakable lessons of successful leaders that Bennis and I, as well as other writers, have documented. Vision and trust, for example, are indispensable to effective leadership but seem to be in short supply today.

But there is an even more basic reason for these failures—the need for a new kind of leadership. *What we currently understand leadership to be is not wrong; it is simply not adequate to the challenge of a new age.* Like an umbrella in a hurricane, the current concept is of some use, but doesn't provide enough coverage. A sturdier structure is needed.

What is missing? We have already suggested where to look. In earlier chapters, we noted that this is a particularly stressful time for Americans. Everywhere around us are accelerating change and uncertainty, global complexity and ambiguity, turbocharged organizational tempos, and instability that comes from perpetual restructuring at the most fundamental level. Nothing is permanent; all is in flux. These are the realities with which the new age of leadership must deal.

When viewed in this context, the current model of leadership seems strangely static. The missing dimension is time. That is to say, the environment, the organization and all its people, are in motion at all times, but not usually in the same direction. The relationships between them are also changing over time.

The new leader must stand at the center of this vibrant dynamic system, acting as both its head and its heart. As its head, the leader must attempt to steer the system through endless storms, scanning the horizon for new threats and opportunities. At the same time, he must redesign the system as it moves along, regulating macroprocesses that determine speed, structure, and direction—processes such as innovation, growth, and improvement. We can call this *visionary leadership*.

As its heart, the leader provides followers with the spiritual and emotional direction we already discussed—common meaning and purpose, trust, empowerment, commitment, and a framework or culture within which to judge what is worth doing and what are acceptable means and ends. In this regard, the leader serves mainly as mentor and role model to help followers understand what is the right thing to do. We can call this *personal leadership.*

The head and the heart are connected, of course, and failure of either leads to quick demise. Even skillful visionary leadership will fail if there is no shared sense of purpose or empowerment to act. Similarly, if a leader does not understand the changing environment or is not capable of moving the system in the right direction, no amount of communication or personal leadership will prevent collapse. I will give the name *futures-creative leadership* to this combination of personal and visionary leadership.

When Martin Luther King set out to revolutionize race relations in America, he was practicing futures-creative leadership. His visionary message ("I have a dream"), combined with the spiritual and emotional call to high purpose and commitment, energized a generation of young followers and profoundly altered the legal, cultural, and institutional structures of American society.

Much less dramatic, but similarly futures-creative, were Edwin Land's pioneering of instant photography and Steve Jobs's leadership of Apple Computer. It can happen at lower levels too, as when a high school teacher led a group of underachieving inner-city kids to a national championship in the academic decathlon, or when a manufacturing manager turned a near-death plant into his firm's most productive facility.

Unfortunately, futures-creative leadership is, by and large, absent in America. The heart has been working normally, but there is a massive headache. People are working harder than ever, but their leaders have not been steering them adequately through our turbulent times. Some doubt that many leaders even understand what is going on, let alone have a clear idea of how to create a better future for their organizations.

In this regard, we should note that it is not the turbulence itself that is to blame. Indeed, if we look back over history we see that leaders are most needed and most valued during times of great change. Moses, Napoleon, Lincoln, Churchill, Mao, and thousands of other men and women whose names are synonymous with great leadership, made their marks precisely when their societies were in flux and often in crisis.

The reason is rather straightforward. In times of stress, an organization or a society is torn in many different directions; people are confused, disoriented, unsure of themselves, and don't know what to expect. They see themselves adrift and may well identify with A. E. Housman's image in "A Shropshire Lad": "I, a stranger and afraid / In a world I never made."

If leaders can provide a sense of direction, if they can transcend the confusion with a convincing model of a greatly improved situation they are trying to create for the future, then they can restore a sense of purpose, catalyze people to act enthusiastically, and align their energies. These images of the future impose meaning and order on the present and serve as a beacon toward which programs can be directed and against which progress can be measured. This in turn can overcome the paralysis and conflict that otherwise inevitably accompany change and uncertainty.

Isn't this just what Americans mean when they talk about the dearth of leadership today? The old visions and metaphors seem tired and worn out, devoid of relevance for what everyone senses is a new age. There is little wonder, then, that today's leaders are unable to inspire commitment and are at a total loss in aligning the energies of followers. Without alignment there is no coherence. Consider national leadership, which seems to point in every direction at once—shipping weapons all over the world in what is billed as a quest for peace; running record budget deficits and tax cuts while claiming to fight inflation; subsidizing tobacco growers while trying to reduce cigarette smoking; allowing the educational system to collapse when the economy can succeed only with technological excellence.

The nation hungers for new direction. Since nothing is more important to modern organizations than their ability to cope with change, nothing is more important for leaders than an understanding of future trends, opportunities, and vulnerabilities. Thus leaders must learn how to become more futures-creative. If the future is the territory in which the American society and its organizations will have to succeed, then we had better learn quickly how to think about it.

5

FUTURES-CREATIVE LEADERSHIP

"Solve the small problem before it becomes big.
The most involved fact in the world
Could have been faced when it was simple,
The biggest problem in the world
Could have been solved when it was small."

—Lao Tzu, *The Way of Life*, 604 B.C.

FOR THE PAST several semesters, I have assigned my students the task of interviewing business leaders at their offices. Among other things, students are asked to probe how futures-creative these leaders seem to be. The students are always able to report a few good examples, but many encounter problems when this subject is raised.

▷Some leaders tell them they are under unbelievable pressure for short-term performance and have little time to devote to the future. But this is just what Lao Tzu warned against 2,500 years ago. If all of a leader's attention is on the short term, then continued crises are almost certain, for he is not taking advantage of lead time to address problems while they are still small.

▷Some leaders say their industries are changing too fast to permit long-range thinking. But it is precisely under these conditions that long-range thinking becomes most necessary to avoid premature obsolescence of products and markets.

▷Some leaders even question whether it is possible to think about the future at all. If we can't predict with any confidence what will happen, why bother?

Behind these expressions of concern lie dangerously antiquated notions of what the future is and how leaders can deal with it. In the next section, I will try to clarify this subject and show how the future can be made a real part of every leader's thinking and action. An extended model of leadership will be described that is suitable for the emerging conditions of the new century.

UNDERSTANDING THE FUTURE

Earlier civilizations believed the gods controlled the future and that humans could do nothing except try to placate the gods and accept their fate. Over centuries, humankind accumulated the skills for influencing nature and shaping the future. However, each age imposed certain limitations. The strength of iron, the force of gravity, the speed of a horse, and the course of a river were all once seen as absolute limits to human activity. One by one, these barriers fell, and they continue to fall with great rapidity. In the past few decades alone, humans have overcome planetary limits and moved into space, synthesized DNA and manipulated genetic materials, penetrated the atom and created solar temperatures, and designed materials superior to any found in nature.

As natural limits fall, the necessity for social choice increases. Once it becomes possible to design key aspects of the human future, it becomes necessary to decide whether and to what extent to do so. Even the decision to take no action has important consequences, so that once an organization becomes capable of shaping its own future, it cannot avoid deciding to do so. The only question is whether futures will be created carefully and well, with due attention to all the consequences of choice, or allowed to happen by default and dealt with after the fact.

Perhaps as a result of this awareness, Americans have a keen interest in the future, as evidenced by instant bestsellers such as *Future Shock* and *Megatrends*. An insatiable audience craves speculation about the future, whether it be in the form of serious scholarship or science fiction or even astrology. There is a field of study called futures research, from which I will draw heavily in this section. Even our vocabulary reflects this interest in the future. It is reported that there are fifty-two words for *snow* in the Eskimo language, but there are at least twice as many words in the English language that refer to the future, a sampling of which is listed in Figure 5.

A unique feature of the human brain is the ability to form mental images of the future and to translate these images into reality through leadership and action. Forces in the outside world impact on a leader's beliefs and values, thereby shaping his images of the future. The leader should constantly anticipate how these forces, current trends, and society's momentum may play out.

These images and expectations determine which issues the leader chooses to address, what goals and means are appropriate in guiding choices, and what he or she views as the most desirable future for the organization or society to pursue. They become embodied in the leader's vision, which is then communicated to followers. Actions taken by followers in response to the intended direction interact with other factors to create a new reality, and the process continues.

FIGURE 5: SOME COMMON WORDS IN A
FUTURE-ORIENTED VOCABULARY

Aim	Foresight	Optimistic	Presentiment
Anticipation	Forestall	Oracle	Presuppose
Aspirations	Foretaste	Outlook	Progress
Conjecture	Foretell	Pessimistic	Projection
Destination	Forethought	Plan	Prolegomenon
Destiny	Foretoken	Portend	Promise
Emerging	Fortune-telling	Posterity	Prophesy
Envision	Forewarn	Potentiality	Prospective
Expectation	Future	Precaution	Prospects
Extrapolation	Futuristics	Precognition	Seer
Forebode	Futurology	Predestination	Soothsayer
Forecast	Goal	Prediction	Speculate
Forejudge	Harbinger	Premonition	Tomorrow
Foreknowledge	Hope	Preparation	Trend
Foreordain	Intention	Presage	Vision
Foresee	Mission	Prescience	Visionary
Foreshadow	Omen	Prescription	Wish

As the leader's mind contemplates the future, he does not attempt to predict what will be. Unlike the past, which one can retrace with a single line of development like Ariadne's thread, there are many alternative futures, each with its associated probability of occurrence. For many areas of interest, it is impossible to enumerate all possible futures. In thinking about energy production in the year 2000, for example, one easily can be overwhelmed by the many possible combinations of coal, oil, natural gas, nuclear energy, fusion, solar, geothermal, waste conversion, chemical, wind, and water power, each of which is influenced in turn by its own combination of political, technical, economic, and industrial forces as they play out over the future.

The leader must generate these images of the future and then sort them into three mental piles. The largest pile, called *possible futures*, includes everything that can evolve from the present state. The articulation of possible futures is a creative act, based on trends, information about the outside world, human imagination, and intuitive insight. For example, a car manufacturer may spend millions on marketing research to understand all the different vehicles and features the public might want in the next decade. This becomes raw material, along with technical and economic studies, the imagination of designers and marketers, and the experience of leaders and managers in the company, for the formulation of a set of possible futures for the industry.

The second pile, called *probable futures*, is smaller because it is a subset of the first, i.e., those possible futures that are seen right now as likely to occur. The assignment of probabilities to possible futures contains a very large judgmental component.

The third pile, the smallest, contains the *preferable futures*, that subset of the possible futures that would lead to desirable outcomes for the organization. It is from these preferred futures that the leader articulates and institutionalizes a set of ideals and missions that become part of his vision for the future of the organization.

Why go through these mental gymnastics? The late Bertrand deJouvenel stated it simply in his classic book, *The Art of Conjecture*: "We often find ourselves trying to bend the course of events in a way that will bring the probable closer to the desirable. And this is the real reason why we study the future." This is the very essence of what we have called futures-creative leadership.

Because there will always be unanticipated changes in the world outside the organization, and because no one can be certain of the human choices that will be made in response to future situations, the future is inherently unpredictable. Thinking about the future will always involve a great deal of uncertainty. In fact, uncertainty increases the further into the future one looks, the more complex or novel the area being considered, and the more dependent it is on human decisions versus natural forces. Labor-management negotiations and new product introductions, for example, have these properties in abundance.

The search for desirable images of the future may actually operate to increase uncertainty by suggesting new options or consequences that had not previously been recognized. A futures-creative leader should embrace this uncertainty because it opens up new possibilities and opportunities; at the same time, too much uncertainty can paralyze an organization. By selecting a direction and promoting a shared sense of purpose in the organization, the leader keeps uncertainty within productive limits.

The leader operates on the future by changing both processes and structures. A process view concentrates the leader's attention on the dynamics of organizations and their environments. By understanding these dynamics, the leader is in a position to apply mid-course corrections to the direction of movement and to steer the organization in a more desirable direction. The head of a government agency, for example, may choose to de-emphasize certain activities in order to free up resources for initiatives in another area.

A structural perspective directs the leader's attention to future states of the organization that are largely determined by internal elements and the way they are organized to interact. In this mode, he is not so much trying to change the system's internal behavior as to redesign its structure to make certain outcomes more likely. For example, the same government agency head may choose to reorganize the agency to give civil servants in the field more decision-making authority.

Any contemplation of alternative images of the future must involve a great deal of judgment and, not infrequently, considerable creativity and intuition as well. There are distinct limits to rational processes in contemplating the future, limits that are soon reached in the face of the complexity and uncertainty that accompany all future states. But this is precisely where the art of leadership must be exercised. Some leaders seem to have extraordinary insight and judgment, carefully cultivated during years of experience and reflection. For example, one airline president was able to draw on thirty years of experience in the business to judge almost instinctively how government regulators, competitors, and the traveling public would respond to a new route configuration.

The raw material for these judgments and images of the future come from three primary sources: information, values, and models.

Information

Many sources of information about the future are readily available, including long-term trends in economics, demography, and resource usage. Often it is possible to detect signals that provide early warning of potential changes in these trends. Planning documents, public-opinion polls, and the stated intentions of policymakers in diverse organizations are also useful in thinking about the future.

A good deal of information about the future can be obtained simply by studying existing societal structures. For example, a mayor thinking about the future of his or her city knows that most of the existing buildings, roads, sewer lines, etc., will still be in use. A political leader might be able to make fairly good judgments about the size, age, and ethnic mix of the voting population in the U.S. election scheduled for the year 2000, since nearly all the potential voters are already known. A business leader could analyze the long-term implications of policies currently being implemented by government and industry leaders.

Finally, all sorts of published forecasts—e.g., environmental impact statements, manpower forecasts, economic projections, and demographic analyses—provide data. Harbingers of future technological developments in today's research laboratories are often reported in technical papers presented at professional meetings or in government and think-tank reports. A vast collection of intellectual ideas that may shape the future—such as political-party platforms, newspaper editorials, speeches by politicians and business leaders, and the writings of social critics and activists—are also easily available.

Indeed, far from being devoid of information about the future, the leader is inundated with it, though only a small part may provide useful benchmarks or signposts. The real art of leadership lies in the interpretation of this information. Just as the historian takes piles of information about the past and constructs an interpretation of what must have happened, so must the leader select, organize, structure, and interpret information about the future in constructing a viable and credible vision. But the leader has one added advantage denied the historian in that much of the future can be invented or designed. His own images of the future are influential in shaping the future itself.

Values

Present and future values are of enormous importance in understanding and managing change. Values impact directly on the choice of possible images of the future to be examined, on the way the images are evaluated and implemented, and on their consequences. Similarly, the leader's own values influence the issues that are addressed in the organization, the information that is sought about the issues, the alternatives that are considered, and the ways in which the alternatives are ordered.

Images of the future reflect values in the large society, in the organization, and in the leader. At the societal level, values like "the American way of life" or conspicuous consumption constitute frames of reference within which social priorities are determined and human relationships are defined.

At the organizational level, values often coalesce into a prevailing ideology that guides that organization's behavior. At American Express, for example, the ideology revolves around a strong commitment to customer service, while the drive for technical excellence and innovation dominates a firm like Microsoft. The organization shapes the ideology of its members through a socialization process that includes training, reward structures, and peer pressure and through the organizational culture that includes heroes, myths, traditions, and "the way we do things here." A compelling and successful vision of the future builds upon the prevailing ideology, and over time may alter it significantly.

For the leader, values provide the criteria for identifying where change is necessary and desirable. He must have a clear understanding of his own values and behave consistently with them—indeed, must personify them—if his visions are to be taken seriously by others.

Models

Values and information, though necessary for the formation of images of the future, are insufficient in and of themselves. Some sort of framework in the leader's mind must determine which alternative images can be tested and evaluated. The more explicit, rational, and orderly the framework or model, the easier it is to understand and refine the image, to communicate it to others with clarity and assurance, and to secure legitimacy for the vision. As systems scientist Sir Geoffrey Vickers has stated:

> Rehearsing possible futures on the stage of the mind, we can play out a dozen alternatives, based on different assumptions, including the assumption of different interventions by ourselves; and we can defer decisions until their probable outcomes have been anticipated and compared. . . . Knowledge gained from such an exercise is sometimes called feedforward, to distinguish it from feedback of actual experience. In all deliberate human action, feedforward plays a far larger direct part than feedback.

Forecasts, the result of this feedforward process, are used for many purposes: to indicate where trends appear to be heading; to suggest areas of change that may need to be faced in the future: to identify limits beyond which alternative futures may not be able to go; to help in evaluating costs and benefits of various alternatives; and to provide a basis upon which decisions to depart from the status quo may be evaluated.

The value and usefulness of this feedforward process can be greatly enhanced if the model can be translated into a language that can be communicated to others. While ordinary natural language eases communication, verbal models contain ambiguities that permit each individual to interpret assumptions and conclusions differently. Sometimes weaknesses can be overcome by blueprints, mock-ups, or mathematical and computer models. Leaders, of course, do not build such models but can employ staff experts for this purpose.

Thus, raw materials for images of the future are provided by information, values, and models. The use of these materials is an art requiring intellectual effort and ingenuity. It is basically a search for understanding and insight, perspective and direction, patterns and relationships, and, ultimately, meaning. Translating this understanding and insight into reality is what futures-creative leadership is all about.

AN EXTENDED MODEL OF LEADERSHIP

Now let's bring the pieces together. Earlier chapters discussed major ways in which our world is changing. Among the most critical changes are elevating technological superiority and global interconnectedness to central concerns on the national agenda; restructuring at every level of society; and accelerating change, choice, risk, and complexity. America has not been coping well with these changes, as measured by the pursuit of its agenda of prosperity/security/happiness.

I have argued that much of the responsibility for failure to adapt to the new realities can be attributed to inadequacies of leadership. At the upper levels, only the leaders of major organizations and institutions have the authority and responsibility to change the system as necessary to make it work better. At lower levels, only effective leadership can redirect the attention of managers and workers to tasks more appropriate to the challenges of the new age and more likely to achieve success.

But why is leadership inadequate? The answer is that the prevailing wisdom about leadership has become danger-ously unbalanced. Leadership is seen as primarily—at times, almost exclusively—concerned with the relationship between the leader and the follower or organization (re-ferred to earlier as personal leadership). Open any book on leadership and most of its contents are devoted to such subjects as communication, trust, empowerment, reward, participation, selection, collaboration, and organizational cultures. All these are important, of course, but even excel-lence in these areas will not close the leadership gap.

The conditions of the new age demand at least as much attention to the ever-changing external environment as to the internal or organizational environment. External envi-ronment does not refer simply to those outside influences that impinge directly on the organization—customers, sup-pliers, and competitors. The larger social, political, eco-nomic, technological, international, and institutional envi-ronments that form the milieu within which an organization functions are at least as important. It is in this larger environment that the major changes have been oc-curring.

Leadership success now requires more attention to the indirect and often ambiguous effects of changes in this larger environment on the operations of the organization. For example, a cereal manufacturer has major concerns beyond customer acceptance, such as government regula-tions on labeling and additives, international competition, agricultural policy, packaging technology, food industry mergers, medical findings on cholesterol, world sugar prices, and foreign exchange rates, to name just a few.

The other reason for the inadequacy of leadership is a preoccupation with the present at the expense of the future. The pace of change is so rapid that present conditions represent only a fleeting and often misleading glimpse of future possibilities. The leader must constantly scan the future horizon because whatever the organization sets out to do today—any commitment, investment, or strategic choice—will have its payoff in the future. The more significant the commitment, the further into the future the payoff is likely to be. Since future circumstances will certainly be very different from those of today, it is important for the leader to understand those circumstances if a correct assessment is to be made about the size and likelihood of any benefits.

Conventional wisdom about leadership often includes vision, but it does so in a way that permits, and sometimes even encourages, mission statements that are little more than a continuation of the status quo. For example, the president of the United States or a corporate leader may have a "vision" of getting back to the basics or cutting the budget. As commendable as these goals may be, they hardly suggest a future distinctly different and better than the present.

A true vision must provide a clear image of a desirable future, one that represents an achievable, challenging, and worthwhile long-range target toward which people can direct their energies. An example would be President Kennedy's vision of a man on the moon by 1970, or a corporate president's vision of a multibillion-dollar global business in superconducting materials.

The new age of leadership requires balanced attention to internal and external environments and to both the present and the future, as suggested in the accompanying diagram.

The leader must be in the center, where it all comes together. It is as if he stands in the middle of a finely woven spider web. If he goes in one direction, he becomes enmeshed in the internal details of the organization, oblivious to changes and new demands in the external environment.

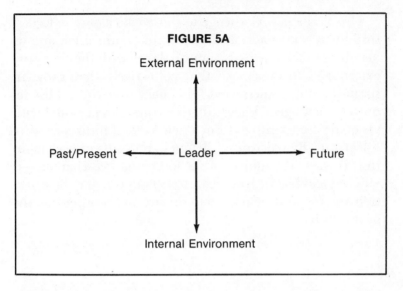

FIGURE 5A

External Environment

Past/Present ←——— Leader ———→ Future

Internal Environment

If he goes in another direction and spends all his time on the outside, sitting on boards of directors and mingling with legislators and other power brokers, he loses touch with his own people. Going down a third path he becomes trapped in history and tradition, so committed to the way things are done here and now that he is unable even to see— much less respond to—the needs of a new age. Going a fourth way, he can be lost in a dreamworld no one shares or cares about. On all these paths, or in any other direction, there is little chance that the organization will be able to prosper, or even to survive, under the rapidly changing, highly uncertain circumstances that will characterize the next ten to twenty years.

Right in the middle of it all. That's where the leader belongs in the new age, balancing the needs of the internal and external environments and the challenges of the present and future. In doing so, the futures-creative leader is also providing a fulcrum for the balance of the micro (analysis, reductionism, subunits) and the macro (synthesis, holism, the big picture); and of the existential (what is) and the normative (what should be).

This is the new challenge to those who aspire to leadership today—to enable a society or an organization and its members to operate in dynamic balance with the changing external environment so that collectively they grow in strength, effectiveness, and legitimacy over time. This requires a new age of leadership that combines personal with visionary leadership to form a new kind of futures-creative leadership. By redefining the roles and skills of leadership in this way—the subject of the following two chapters—it will be possible for American leaders to provide the direction and inspiration needed to survive and prosper into the next century.

6

LEADERSHIP ROLES

"Any path which narrows future possibilities may become a lethal trap. Humans are not threading their way through a maze; they scan a vast horizon filled with unique opportunities. The narrowing viewpoint of the maze should appeal only to creatures with their noses buried in sand."

—Frank Herbert, *Children of Dune*

NAPOLEON BONAPARTE, WHO rose to leadership in a period of great change and turmoil, may have been an early pioneer of futures-creative leadership. Seizing the moment, he inspired his troops to incredible victories over the nations of central Europe and came close to gathering all of Europe under his rule. As first consul and then emperor of France, he united his country following the excesses of the French Revolution, introduced a new legal system, greatly improved the economic condition of the French people, and stimulated the arts and sciences.

Here's how a contemporary biographer, Louis Madelin,

described Napoleon's thinking process:

> He would deal with three or four alternatives at the same time and endeavor to conjure up every possible eventuality—preferably the worst. This foresight, the fruit of meditation, generally enabled him to be ready for any setback; nothing ever took him by surprise. . . . His vision . . . was capable of both breadth and depth. Perhaps the most astonishing characteristic of his intellect was the combination of idealism and realism which enabled him to face the most exalted visions at the same time as the most insignificant realities. And indeed, he was in a sense a visionary, a dreamer of dreams.

More than a visionary, Napoleon was also skilled in personal leadership. He was a master at communicating his vision so that his audience would become electrified by it, compelled even to the point of being willing to die for it. Sensitivity to his followers is demonstrated in many of his famous sayings, such as, "The art of choosing men is not nearly as difficult as the art of enabling those one has chosen to attain their full worth" and "Without doubt, the first duty of the ruler is to do what the people want."

Napoleon knew how to use the traditions of the past ("the glory that was France") and the human energies of the present to create the future he envisioned. As long as he skillfully practiced futures-creative leadership, he could, and did, change the world. When he finally failed as a leader, it was because, not shy about his own genius, he allowed ego and ambition to blur his vision.

Like Napoleon, successful leaders today must enthuse their followers, align their energies toward new directions, and create a new future for their organizations and for society. Doing this means that the futures-creative leader must be prepared to assume certain roles.

THE WORK OF THE
FUTURES-CREATIVE LEADER

For the futures-creative leader, the future is not some
never-never land; it very much exists in the mind, much as
the North Pole exists in the mind, although few of us have
been there. And because it exists it influences the principal
roles the leader is expected to fulfill: direction-setter,
change agent, spokesperson, and coach.

Direction-Setter

Casey Stengel once said, "If you don't know where you're
going, you might end up somewhere else." As direction-
setter, the leader is called upon to point the way, to be the
champion of a particular image of what is possible, desirable, and intended for the future of a collective effort. The
reasons for this have been often addressed:

> There is . . . no future other than as we will it to be. If
> we conceive of a future state as desirable, we tend to
> orient ourselves toward it and to initiate the courses of
> action necessary to its attainment. (McHale, 1969)

> There are many advantages to powerful determination
> and a strong sense of direction. The sense of direction
> urges action. The sense of direction shapes the action.
> The sense of direction allows the value of the action to
> be assessed: has it got me nearer my goal? The sense of
> direction allows all judgments and decisions to be
> made more easily: does this help me toward my goal or
> hinder me? (deBono, 1984)

> To grasp and hold a vision, to fix it in your senses, that
> is the very essence, I believe, of successful leadership.
> Not only on the movie set, where I learned it, but
> everywhere. (Ronald Reagan, May 31, 1988)

This vision of the future may be expressed as a dream, an agenda, a mission statement, a challenge, or a sense of purpose. "Let's go that way," says the leader, "and together we'll all be able to realize our own deepest desires for meaning, accomplishment, and self-fulfillment. There is where the action is, where we can make our unique contribution. On that path lie the glittering prizes."

History provides many examples of great leaders whose unique and powerful visions of the future guided organizations and entire nations to great effort and accomplishments. These leaders were captivated by their dreams and obsessed with the need to turn them into reality. They were able to infect others with enthusiasm and commitment to their visions, until a critical mass shared the dream. Once that happens the vision already has become a reality as a motivator of behavior, and all that remains is to give the dream tangible form.

Modern leaders also know the importance of direction-setting—which explains why Yassir Arafat declared an independent Palestinian state and why Steve Jobs set such high performance goals for the Next computer. Even at much lower organizational levels—the director of a research project, the local sales manager, the foreman on a production line, the coach of a baseball team—direction-setting is the principal means by which leaders energize and inspire common efforts.

The role of direction-setting never ceases because the environment changes. As new opportunities and challenges appear, some parts of the dream may be realized while others are shown to be no longer feasible. The leader is constantly reassessing the vision, refining it, allowing it to evolve and grow. While we have been in the habit of thinking of the leader as the Lone Ranger, we really should have been paying more attention to his alter ego Tonto, the scout who shows the way.

Change Agent

The futures-creative leader is literally a designer of the future, out to change the world in some significant way. Edwin Land changed the way we think about photography; Walt Disney redesigned the amusement park; Jimmy Carter helped change the relationship between Israel and Egypt; and Betty Friedan reconceptualized the role of women in America. In all these cases the leader not only pointed toward a new direction but acted to change the rules of the game.

People will resist change if they don't understand its purpose, if they feel it will affect them or the organization adversely, or if they feel it is being imposed arbitrarily. The futures-creative leader knows this and builds an organizational climate that welcomes change by encouraging mutual caring, trust, open communication, and participation.

The leader as change agent acts by making critical decisions, using his position of authority to make important choices, i.e., the decision to invest in a new process, to build a new facility, to call a strike, or to acquire another company. Other times the leader may be a change agent by influencing the choices of others—when a senator builds a coalition to pass a piece of legislation or a corporate leader secures a zoning concession from a local government, for example.

In addition to changing the world, the futures-creative leader is also the designer of his or her own organization, often having final responsibility for choosing which constituencies an organization shall serve, which issues to address, which objectives are consistent with the chosen direction, and which outside organizations are to be competitors or joint partners. He or she builds his or her own leadership team, makes policy, approves or vetoes personnel or financial decisions made by others, and often is called upon to resolve conflicts.

The leader has ultimate responsibility for the design of the organizational culture—rules, moral code, structures, rituals, information flows, and decision processes that together determine what is legitimate and desirable inside the organization. Teamwork and cooperation must be designed into the organization. That is, if there is to be a good fit among the evolving capabilities of the organization, the ever-changing external environment, and the intended direction, then the leader is the key change agent who must make it happen.

Spokesperson

Futures-creative leadership is strongly involved in brokering the needs of constituencies both inside and outside the organization. More and more of the decisions made by leaders are public decisions; that is, they affect people who insist on being heard. The bigger the issue to be tackled, the more power is diffused and the more people have to be involved. Leaders have to cope with the politicization of all institutions, which means mobilizing public opinion, working more closely with state and local governments, and being "more public" in conducting the affairs of the enterprise. No longer can the role of spokesperson be delegated to an external affairs department.

Recently, the media has emerged as a major part of the external environment, available not only to leaders but to critics and supporters as well. Therefore leaders must be able to articulate the organization's viewpoint. They also must be able to listen to and take action based on feedback through the media from relevant stakeholders.

As spokesperson, the leader is the ceremonial head *and* the organization's agent in interactions and negotiations with other organizations and the media. It works in the other direction as well. The leader's reputation outside the organization tends to support his standing within. He is often called on to explain the significance of outside developments and constituencies to followers in the organization, thereby bridging the internal and external environments.

The leader is a spokesperson in another sense as well; he is a sort of ombudsman for the future, the advocate for future needs and constituencies. The future needs representation in the present, especially when current challenges and crises are consuming the attention and energies of an organization. Japanese business leaders do this particularly well, keeping attention focused on distant goals such as market position and penetration even at the cost of near-term profits. This will be discussed further in Chapter 12.

Coach

The futures-creative leader serves as coach by being a mentor and role model for the organization. As such, he must embody and demonstrate the characteristics he believes are most important for the future of the organization. Consider the following examples:

▷Moving into a situation at Chrysler that many had considered hopeless, Lee Iacocca provided the model for others to emulate—innovative, competent, future-oriented, pragmatic, open to advice from all directions, enthusiastic, and committed. He was able to infuse Chrysler with his zeal for not only finding a way out of that firm's dire circumstances but for opening a way into a viable long-term position in the automotive marketplace.

▷One of the students of violinist Jascha Heifetz said he never felt he was doing well in his class, not when compared with the master. But Heifitz, like all great coaches, encouraged his students to set their own standards for judging themselves. His many protégés attest to his success in doing so.

▷After building MTM into one of the most successful television production companies of his time, Grant Tinker went to NBC when the network was suffering and raised its profits nearly tenfold in five years. Now he runs his own company again. In each job, he developed a reputation as a fine coach, able to enrich everyone with whom he came into contact.

The leader is there not to use other people but to serve them. As with any good coach, the job of the leader is to discover which followers need help and then see that they get it. The basic assumption, proven time and again in academic studies and polls, is that people want to do a good job, make a difference, and find meaning in their work. As coach, the leader helps them to grow and to reach their true potential.

No organization or social movement can do its best unless its members are doing their best, both individually and collectively. The leader cannot order them to do their best but can challenge, inspire, and show them ways to improve. Ultimately, followers discover their own best ways of contributing. Therefore, the coaching role is basically a form of guided self-discovery.

Among the characteristics the leader as coach must instill into the organization, none is more critical than the set of ethics and norms that define good and bad, right or wrong in the behavior of the group. Leaders can establish a set of ethics by demonstrating their personal commitment to them through their own behavior. Martin Luther King served as a living example to everyone in the civil rights movement of a coherent set of moral principles related to justice, self-sacrifice, conscience, nonviolence, and duty.

Thus, the futures-creative leader lives the future in the present, creating hope and high expectations for those who otherwise would founder under their own and the organization's weaknesses and vulnerabilities. As coach the leader is teacher, learner, facilitator, role model, and friend. By showing that people really do matter, the coach/leader builds the organization into an instrument for changing the future.

These four roles—direction-setter, change agent, spokesperson, and coach—are the key to futures-creative leadership and meeting the leadership demands of the new age. Together they provide the answer to exploding uncertainty, change, and complexity. Uncertainty is reduced by removing ambiguity about intentions and by having consistently ordered priorities. Adaptation to change is facilitated by designing responsive organizations and igniting the commitment of followers. Complexity is made manageable when all constituencies, both in and outside the organization, understand what it stands for and what norms guide its behavior.

These are matters of the greatest substance, as they lay out the agenda, the intentions, and the rationale for the future of the enterprise. In doing so, they clarify the work of everyone who has a duty to perform and yet allow considerable scope for action in the choice of methods, people, resources, and technologies to be employed.

But how can leaders be effective in these roles? The facile formulas of pop writers seem singularly useless. "Be charismatic," they say. "Dress for success. Surround yourself with good people and delegate well. Promote participation." None of these seems to get at the essence of the principal roles discussed here. The truth is, there are no shortcuts to futures-creative leadership, no "one-minute leader." Those who aspire to leadership must earn the right to lead. This can be done by developing the seven special competencies to which we now turn our attention.

7

THE SEVEN MEGASKILLS

"If it be now, 'tis not to come;
if it be not to come, it will be now;
if it be not now, yet it will come:
the readiness is all."

—William Shakespeare, *Hamlet*

WHEN LEADERS WRITE about their leadership or give advice to others, they nearly always focus on qualities— determination, ambition, sensitivity, competitiveness, sense of humor, optimism, and so forth. When *Fortune* ran its lead article on October 24, 1988, entitled "The Seven Keys to Business Leadership," it listed things leaders should do— trust subordinates, develop vision, keep your cool, encourage risk, be an expert, invite dissent, simplify.

Apart from developing vision, I find these combined bits of advice unsatisfying and not very useful in understanding how to develop leadership. They are unsatisfying because it is easy to think of leaders who did not have a particularly good sense of humor or leaders who were far from being experts in the areas they led. Often circumstances are such that further risk should not be encouraged, and simple answers frequently fall short in a complex situation.

The suggestions are not useful because they don't help a leader improve his performance. Surely success in leadership will not come simply by being more ambitious or likable, or by inviting dissent or keeping cooler.

Worst of all, these simplistic notions don't offer insight into what is needed to lead in the complex, rapidly changing global environment we see before us. Instead, we need to take a closer look at leadership skills or abilities; we need to develop a job description for a futures-creative leader.

I have coined the word *megaskills* to capture the notion of a family of interrelated skills. These megaskills, seven in all, are essential to success at futures-creative leadership. Discussed briefly here, they are illustrated in the following four chapters.

Farsightedness

The minds of futures-creative leaders must operate in the future tense, always searching for possible opportunities and threats, always asking "What if?" and "Why not?" and "So what?" Such minds pay attention to past and present primarily to determine their implications for the future.

Farsightedness means keeping the eye firmly fixed on the far horizon, even as one takes steps toward it. Consider, for example, the way director Peter Brook describes his leadership:

> Of course, there are some good English actors who would become paralyzed if you changed anything after the first day. Naturally, they are not the actors I can work with. But when I worked with John Gielgud or Orson Welles, for example, they would have been appalled if I had come to work with a rigid plan. What I do is study until something grows which is a sense of direction, which is knowing what one is looking for—

that it is over there, on the other side of the mountain. But there are many paths to get to the other side of the mountain and perhaps all of them must be tried. Directing is pointing, not imposing. Someone asks you for the way, you direct them. If they set off misunderstanding you, you stop them and say no, and point in the right direction.

Farsightedness gives the leader the perspective necessary to form a vision, the driving dream that embodies his intentions and serves as a beacon for others in the organization. It is indispensable in direction-setting. By giving the future a tangible reality as a target or purpose, farsightedness becomes a real force in guiding the present.

Farsightedness has other benefits as well. It helps the leader think about the long-range consequences of current actions and choices. It may provide early notice of issues and opportunities worth exploring. It may suggest new options of which he was not previously aware or provide reasons why currently favored directions may not be viable in the long term.

This does not mean leaders are fortune-tellers. The mental process is more like that of a historian skilled in collecting facts and then interpreting change by tracing cause-and-effect relationships as they played out over a period of time. Using his imagination to fill the gaps, the historian tries to describe what "really" happened, why it happened, and why it was important.

The future offers no similar facts but, as discussed in Chapter 5, there is plenty of raw material with which to work. Like the historian, the leader has a mental model of cause-and-effect relationships built up over years of experience, training, reading, and reflection. Using this mental model of how the world works, he can evaluate current trends and possible developments for their long-term significance.

Farsightedness stimulates the creative, imaginative, and

intuitive processes that are essential in direction-setting. The end result of this process is vision, which is composed of equal portions of farsightedness and insight.

Nothing narrows the vision and impoverishes an organization so much as a leader locked into an image of the future as a perpetuation of the present. To stand still, or simply do more of the same, is a formula for disaster under the circumstances we have been discussing. Indeed, it is the very opposite of futures-creative leadership.

Mastery of Change

Many Americans have a simple sense of optimism that all problems have solutions. The more complex the world, the less this is true. Any attempt to "solve" problems such as toxic waste or new product introduction has hundreds of reverberations and endless boomerang effects. The problem is not likely to be solved for long, and frequently new problems are triggered.

Instead of trying to solve problems leaders must treat them as dynamic situations, subject to streams of decisions designed to transform or contain them. Like surfers, dancers, and basketball players, leaders must be keenly aware of the fluidity of an evolving situation, of the constant movement in the environment that surrounds it, and of the degrees of freedom to shape both the situation and the environment. This is how the leader steers growth and transformation in the organization.

Every organization operates and evolves in the midst of a stream of events. For some, like IBM or Texas Instruments, the stream of events moves rapidly and jerkily, with frequent short spurts. At the other extreme are tradition-bound societies in which the stream of events may move so slowly that each year looks very much like the one just past, and fundamental change may be measured in generations. By the same token, there is a pace and tempo to the internal operations of an organization, most conspicuously in the stream of information flow and the rhythm of decision making. For example, contrast the pace of decision making at an urban newspaper with that of the Catholic church.

The leader is responsible for regulating the speed, direction, and rhythm of the organization so that its growth and evolution matches the external pace of events. To some extent, of course, this happens automatically. As the pace of external change speeds up, the demand on the organization for responsiveness also speeds up. This is easily observed in a department store, where the pace is relatively slow during normal times but becomes supercharged during the Christmas rush.

Ensuring flexibility of response is not the only challenge confronting leaders. It may be possible to affect the speed of events in the external environment directly. A field commander can slow down or speed up the pace of engagements with the enemy. A business executive can accelerate new product introductions, which will push competitors to do the same. An environmentalist or civil rights leader can file more lawsuits. However, this can only be done within limits. Leaders in the U.S. automobile industry discovered that they were unable to slow down the transition to smaller, more fuel-efficient cars after the OPEC oil crisis of the mid-seventies. Nonetheless, some dimensions often exist within which the pace of change in the external environment can be influenced.

The futures-creative leader can also operate much like a canoeist, choosing the streams in which to ply his craft. A clothing manufacturer can choose to operate at the high-fashion end of business where change is rapid, risks are high, and firms can make or lose huge profits in a single season. On the other hand, the manufacturer could produce staples that change little from year to year, such as work clothes. Although risk is reduced, so is the potential for high returns.

Similarly, most products and services operate on a three-phase life cycle: rapid change during the early period; a long period of decelerating change and stability; eventual decline. Here again, the leader can position the organization on the slower or faster part of the life cycle, with commensurate risks and opportunities. A furniture maker, for example, could make either kitchen tables or desks for personal computers with almost the same equipment and technology. In large organizations such choices are encountered frequently, where the leader must select an appropriate portfolio of products and services to balance the risk associated with slow- and fast-moving environments.

These examples illustrate another point as well. One of the important skills in mastering change is ability to control uncertainty, which comes from:

- What is truly unknown
- What is seen to be completely or partly uncontrollable
- What is not understood
- Emerging situations that are unprecedented
- Accelerating change that produces frequent surprises
- Failure to examine the consequences of possible actions

If left unattended, uncertainty can cause anxiety, organizational paralysis, and arrested growth and change.

Remember, however, that high levels of uncertainty are to be expected; they cannot be reduced significantly, even with the most advanced information systems. The leader must not only be comfortable in the face of uncertainty but must be able to transcend it by increasing his understanding of future possibilities and setting the level of risks to be taken. Moreover, because uncertainty virtually assures that some decisions will turn out wrong, the leader must carefully assemble a balanced portfolio of risks, be alert in monitoring change, and be skilled at damage control.

The effective leader knows that the future belongs to those in motion. Organizations are like jet aircraft—difficult to get off the ground but relatively easy to redirect once in motion. The futures-creative leader steers growth and transformation by regulating processes such as new product introduction, risk taking, and decision making. Unlike the aircraft pilot, however, he must also repair and redesign the organization while it is in motion.

Organization Design

The instrument with which the leader creates the future is the organization, institution, or social movement he heads. The skills needed to design that instrument are much like the skills an architect uses in designing a home. Basically, they are as follows:

1. Determining the human context. In designing a house, the architect first studies the family's needs, lifestyle, and desires; their dreams, tastes, values, and priorities. Just so, the leader must understand the human context for the evolving organization. What will it need to accomplish for the realization of the intended future? Can these values and priorities best be realized through formal structures and rules, or would a team approach be better? To what extent should people be hired or selected for creativity, professional competence, or other attributes (flexibility, responsiveness, ability to grow, compatibility, accomplishments, ambitions, etc.)?

2. Establishing policy guidelines. Next, the architect works with the family to establish design parameters—house size, style, budget, completion date. Policies are determined for how contractors will be chosen, who will make the detailing decisions, how much emphasis on aesthetics versus utility, etc. Similarly, the leader establishes many policy guidelines—performance criteria such as desired rates of return or cost constraints, professional standards, ethical norms, and employee guidelines.

3. Fixing the setting. The architect may help with site

selection, matching the site to various needs (proximity to schools and parks, security, zoning, geological structures, and the like), and placing the house on the site (landscaping, access, relation to neighboring properties, and views). The leader also must design the setting, including the organization's boundaries; its relationships with suppliers, clients, and other constituencies; accessibility; and so forth.

4. Designing the structures and support systems. The architect next designs various physical structures, such as rooms, windows, and doors; support systems, such as plumbing and electrical; environmental systems, such as heating and cooling; and human-oriented systems, such as decorative features and room views. The leader also designs structures and systems, some of which define roles and relationships, as in organizational charts, networks, and chains of command. Some define information and communication flows, while others establish rituals, such as procedures for approving investment proposals. Some involve entire organizational cultures.

5. Implementation. Finally, with the design completed, the architect prepares detailed drawings and may follow through to obtain permits, assist in the choice of contractors, check on workmanship, and make design adjustments as necessary. So, too, does the leader end the design process by helping to implement the design through staffing decisions, following through on performance, and making design adjustments as needed.

Thus, the futures-creative leader needs design skills of a high order, as the leader is, quite literally, an institution-builder whose legacy is an organization capable of success in realizing the desired vision.

Anticipatory Learning

Learning has always been an important part of leadership, for it is the light that illuminates new ideas, understanding, and insights. Every leader is a lifelong learner and is committed to promoting organizational learning as well. Every leader understands his own strengths and weaknesses and is able to learn from failures and successes. The new ability required by futures-creative leadership is to learn not only from actual experiences but, especially, from anticipations of the future. As the Queen said in *Through the Looking Glass*, "It's a poor sort of memory that only works backward."

In forming anticipations of the future the leader starts with an understanding of the present and past. This understanding may have come from personal observation, works of scholarship or critical commentary, or conversations with colleagues. To keep the understanding fresh and relevant, he often watches trends and indicators that suggest emerging problems or opportunities or that help in understanding how the world works. Like a doctor monitoring a patient's vital signs, the leader watches trends to learn how the condition of the economy or society may be changing.

Trends also can be projected into the future to form a sort of baseline set of expectations of what might occur if the current momentum is sustained without interruption. For example, a leader in the personal computer field might project industry sales based on the last ten years to develop an image of what possible demand might be in the next decade. However, he knows that trend is not unalterable, so he also studies discontinuities that could disrupt the trend line. For example, there might be technical breakthroughs such as voice-input computers; economic effects like a change in the tax deductibility of home computers; new applications such as remedial reading in classrooms; or a host of other developments.

In addition to continuities and discontinuities, the effect of human intervention should be considered. For example, competitors may change distribution methods, or potential customers may decide they don't need to purchase the latest computer devices. By considering possible human intervention, the leader learns about the interests of various constituencies and then imagines the various scenarios that might result, thus assessing their implications for his own agenda.

Chapter 5 reviewed the abundant information about the future available to the alert leader. By considering this information, making judgments about possible and probable futures that may occur, and then updating these images constantly as new information becomes available, the leader gains the following advantages:

- He learns what is important, where he is vulnerable, and which constituents may need attention.

- He enriches his own understanding of how the world works and learns what to watch for early warning of future developments.

- He develops a clearer picture of sources of uncertainty and thus may be able to reduce unpleasant surprises in the future.

- He may learn of new options or at least will be better able to assess the consequences of actions already contemplated.

- He learns how much lead time is available for decision making and what might follow from failure to act in time.

Such forward-directed or anticipatory learning supplements traditional learning based on studies of past performance or current conventional wisdom. Together they provide the early warning, insights, and comprehension needed to sharpen the leader's judgments about what needs to be done now to prepare for, and to create, the future.

Initiative

The traditional test for leadership is whether the candidate has a "track record" that demonstrates an ability to make things happen; everyone values a winner. The futures-creative leader must exercise the same initiative, decisiveness, determination, and follow-through expected of all good leaders. In addition, however, special skills are needed to fulfill the change-agent role, skills normally associated with entrepreneurship and innovation.

What the futures-creative leader makes happen literally changes the world in any number of ways. One way is by building new niches in a marketplace, as Apple Computer did by inventing a market for home computers or Sony did with the Walkman. Another is by setting a new standard of service, quality, or customer satisfaction, thereby altering the expectations of users and forcing competitors to respond. Still another way is by differentiating the organization so much that it appears to have a position of uniqueness, à la Rolls-Royce or Kentucky Fried Chicken.

What are the skills needed to create new niches, set a new service standard, or differentiate an organization? Every organization, public or private, serves some clientele. The futures-creative leader can see the world as his client does, can "feel" the client's intentions, frustrations, and needs. This comes from being sensitive to environmental signals; from being curious, inquisitive, and genuinely interested in what the client has to say; from seeking constant feedback and being a super listener when a signal comes. Polls, surveys, and market research may provide useful inputs, but only to the leader who can empathize with clients, customers, or constituents. When a presidential candidate or a large corporation loses in a competitive struggle, it can often be traced to losing touch with key constituents through overreliance on statistical aggregates.

Like an acupressurist, the futures-creative leader knows where the sensitive spots are in an organization and where to exert pressure to make things happen. He has a keen ability to separate the critical from the merely interesting, often jumping on opportunities that offer leverage in moving the organization forward, while foregoing or delegating issues of lesser importance. A restless experimenter, the futures-creative leader is perfectly willing to accept the failure of many small tests to gain knowledge of which way to proceed. He knows that some pilot projects will fail, and while always alert to cutting losses when necessary, he also knows that in these failures lie the seeds of understanding how to succeed for the long run.

In a world of explosive technological change the leader also must generate and sustain an exceptional pace of technological change within the organization. This means devoting a good deal of personal attention to the developmental side of the organization—assuring that first-rate technical people are hired and given proper working conditions; investing in laboratories and pilot plants; facilitating technology transfers among various parts of the organization; and recognizing and rewarding technological accomplishments. Most of all it means being an advocate for constant innovation. Here, as in many other cases, the leader can serve as a role model by using the latest technologies himself, as appropriate; by celebrating technical progress in speeches and advertising; and by keeping personally up to date on the state of the art of relevant technologies.

The ability to rapidly and creatively adapt ideas used elsewhere is another useful skill for the leader who wants to make new things happen. There is nothing novel in this, of course. Trade associations have served for many years to disseminate ideas that work elsewhere. Every small retailer knows that suppliers and competitors often provide great ideas on what lines to carry or how to improve displays. The Japanese have shown that the new global interdependence requires extending this idea internationally.

Finally, the futures-creative leader is able to entertain unconventional organizational arrangements. When General Motors proposed the joint NUMMI project with Toyota and acquired Hughes to gain an advanced electronics capability, that was innovative leadership of a high order and a welcome change from years of plodding along a conventional and downward path. Similarly, when American

Hospital Supply Corporation extended its own boundaries by installing desk terminals for each of its customers and linking them to its own information system, it reached new levels of service and responsiveness while creating barriers for competitors marketing to the same hospitals. The ability to search for, recognize, and embrace these new organizational arrangements is essential for the leader who means to change the world.

Mastery of Interdependence

Americans have always believed strongly in self-reliance and competitiveness, characteristics that no doubt stimulate affluence. Lately, however, this has exacted a high price. Competitiveness isolates people by making some winners and others losers. It drives people to make ethical compromises, undermines their sense of community, and causes an excessive preoccupation with self at others' expense.

In a complex, highly interdependent world, cooperation is much more important than competition. This may shock believers in the "law of the jungle" and "survival of the fittest." It turns out, however, that even in biological systems, creatures adapt best by finding mutually supportive and adaptive ecological niches.

So it is at every level—international, national, regional, interorganizational, and intraorganizational—including directly competitive business enterprises. As an example, considering football as an economic enterprise, the greatest forces for its success have been cooperative rather than competitive, despite the carnage on the playing field. Examples of cooperative behavior include forming and enforcing common rules, orderly sharing of the television market, franchise restrictions, college draft agreements, and collaboration with advertisers and city governments. Most businesses employ a variety of legal cooperative arrangements, including lobbying by trade associations, cross-licensing agreements, joint ventures, industrywide collective bargaining, technology sharing at professional meetings, local networks of managers, and informal sharing of information through suppliers, former employees, consultants, and customers.

Dean Tjosvold explains why cooperation is superior to competition as follows:

> In cooperation, people realize that they are successful when others succeed and are oriented toward aiding each other to perform effectively. They encourage each other because they understand the other's priorities help them to be successful. Compatible goals promote trust. People expect help and assistance from others and are confident that they can rely on others; it is, after all, in others' self interest to help. Expecting to get and give assistance, they accurately disclose their intentions and feelings, offer ideas and resources, and request aid. They are able to work out arrangements of exchange that leave all better off. These interactions result in friendliness, cohesion, and high morale.
>
> Competitors, by contrast, recognize that others' successes threaten and frustrate their own aspirations. They are closer to reaching their goals when others perform ineffectively and fail to reach theirs. They suspect that others will not help them, for to do so would only harm their own chances of goal attainment. Indeed, they may be tempted to try to mislead and interfere in order to better reach their own goals. They are reluctant to discuss their needs and feelings or to ask for or offer assistance. Closed to being influenced by the other for fear of being exploited, they doubt that they can influence others, except by coercion and threat. These interactions result in frustration, hostility, and low productivity, especially in joint tasks.

Futures-creative leadership demands the willing and enthusiastic cooperation of people and other organizations in a joint effort to create something new and better. The leader must be able to inspire others to share ideas, trust, and commitment; to communicate well and frequently; and to seek collaborative solutions to problems that will permit the organization to grow, change, and constantly improve. This is done by negotiating and building coalitions; by furthering participation in decision making and ownership of the results; and by personal example of shared concern, trust, and respect. It is clear when leaders are successful at fostering collaboration, as noted in the following examples:

- When band leader Woody Herman died, Nat Pierce, a pianist and composer who worked with him off and on for many years, said, "We never felt we were working for him. We were always working *with* him."
- John F. Kennedy was so adept at fostering collaboration that he was able to convert many in the Washington press corps, traditionally the bane of U.S. presidents, into "friends" who treated his administration kindly and with respect even while reporting on its tribulations.
- Jim Robinson, CEO of American Express Company, has been quoted as saying, "I'm not as smart as a lot of people by a long shot, but I thoroughly enjoy getting smart people around me, and often I can pull together a consensus better than they can."

Nothing is so energizing as a leader who is able to forge talented individuals into a team for which each is willing to do his very best for the collective good.

High Standards of Integrity

Dag Hammarskjöld was revered as secretary-general of the United Nations during some of its tumultuous formative years. He was also remarkably introspective, as the world learned with the posthumous publication of his diary, titled *Markings*. Here, then, are some thoughts of a world leader about what it means to lead:

Only he deserves power who every day justifies it.

Never, for the sake of peace and quiet, deny your own experience or convictions.

A task becomes a duty from the moment you suspect it to be an essential part of that integrity which entitles a man to assume responsibility.

In any human situation, it is cheating not to be, at every moment, one's best. How much more so in a position where others have faith in you.

Your position never gives you the right to command. It only imposes on you the duty of so living your life that others can receive your orders without being humiliated.

A leader without trust is like a bird without wings, a pathetic creature able to do little but strut about for a time, weak and vulnerable, accomplishing little and soon displaced. There can be no trust unless the leader is trustworthy—dependable and reliable, honest and honorable. This has always been true, but those who aspire to futures-creative leadership must aim for an even higher standard.

The conditions of change described in earlier chapters suggest that today's accepted moral standards are inadequate for the next two decades. With rapid technological change, societal restructuring, and the globalization of issues and institutions, the futures-creative leader must learn how to embody and inculcate both traditional and new moral imperatives or be accused of being out of step with the emerging reality.

Traditional imperatives include fairness, honesty, tolerance, dependability, caring, openness, loyalty, mutual respect, and commitment to the best traditions of the past.

The new ethical imperatives, which will be discussed in the next chapter, have more to do with keeping faith with the future: caring about what the organization and its members can become and do; being dedicated to improvement and progress; and preventing damage to innocent third parties, such as consumers, local communities, and the environment.

Leaders need to stop acting as if everything is all right as long as they don't violate the law. Skirting along the edge of the law presumes that there are no consequences to immoral behavior. On the contrary, there are many penalties, not least of which are the costs of the small army of auditors, inspectors, and attorneys needed to keep such organizations from self-destructing. Also, there are grievous organizational costs associated with distrust and loss of respect. Wary of change and cynical about the real intentions of leaders, people avoid commitment and find it difficult to muster the enthusiasm to do their best for the organization.

In short, those who would exercise leadership must see themselves as having undertaken a sacred trust. Their vision and actions must at all times be ethical and, occasionally, even ennobling. Otherwise they won't earn the trust they need to operate. People want to be uplifted and will not continue to support a fraud. They will, however, forgive mistakes by a leader they believe to be honest, fair, and trustworthy.

SUMMING UP

In this chapter we have described seven megaskills required of the futures-creative leader. All of these skills (and the roles discussed in the prior chapter) are interrelated and mutually reinforcing, as shown in Figure 6. Farsightedness without integrity is incapable of inspiring trust. Mastery of interdependence without the ability to make things happen is powerless to change the future. A coach without anticipatory learning is unprepared for the challenges to come.

When all the elements are present, however, the leader has unparalleled opportunities to shape the future. In the next four chapters, we'll see how these elements provide the key to improving leadership at the individual, organizational, and national levels, adding up to a cultural renaissance that may well be called the new age of leadership.

FIGURE 6: LEADERSHIP ROLES AND SKILLS

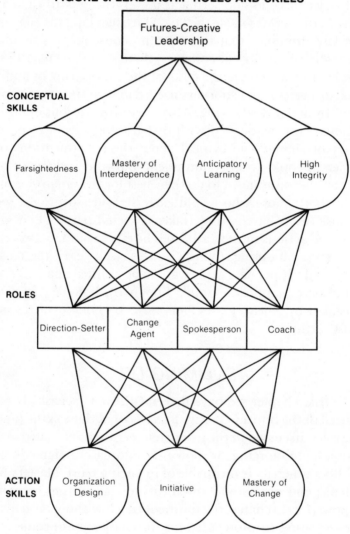

8

THE LEADER'S EDGE

"We are the music makers
And we are the dreamers of dreams . . .
Yet we are the movers and shakers
Of the world forever, it seems."

—Arthur O'Shaughnessy,
  "Music and Moonlight," 1874

AS A BUSINESS school professor for the past twenty years, I have faced many potential "movers and shakers" in my classes and executive seminars. This chapter is for them, and for you, if you are one of the thousands in organizations large and small, at every level, who have the talent and ambition for leadership.

Look around and you will see that America has the room—indeed, a desperate need—for millions of new leaders in the next decade. None of these leaders will be divinely chosen; they all will have to learn to lead, whether they create their own organizations from scratch or are promoted into leadership. All will learn on the job, for leaders are self-designed individuals. They fashion their leadership skills from the countless positive and negative choices they make, from the demands and opportunities they meet, and from the conflicts and victories they experience along the way.

According to a series of research studies by Morgan McCall and his colleagues at the Center for Creative Leadership, there were sixteen developmental experiences that made a lasting difference in the careers of 191 successful leaders from six major corporations. Five were based on assignments—building something from nothing; fixing a failing operation; participating in an important task force; increasing responsibility for people, dollars, or functions; and moving from line to staff roles. Two derived from other people—learning from a role model and observing how others handled an important challenge. Five involved learning from hardships—business failures and mistakes; job rejection; disciplining a subordinate; taking on a new career challenge; and personal traumas that served to stimulate reappraisal of personal values. The other three were early work experiences; the first time managing people; and experiences outside work. Only one of the sixteen developmental experiences had to do with formal course work.

So leaders learn to lead mainly on the job. But what if, as argued in earlier chapters, the world is changing so fast that experience provides only a limited guide for the future? And what if new skills are needed for futures-creative leadership, skills less useful in the past or right now than they will be in a few short years? And what if, on top of all that, the new megaskills require new modes of seeing and thinking, or new kinds of information more attuned to feedforward than to feedback?

In the future, experience will not be enough. What the aspiring leader *does* with the experience—how it is supplemented and interpreted—will determine how prepared he will be.

TAKING THE HIGH ROAD

In the novel *The Chosen*, a boy tells his friend about his grandfather who, as rabbi in a small town in southern Russia, led his people on a perilous five-month journey through Russia, Austria, France, and England to arrive at Ellis Island. The friend is amazed as the dialogue proceeds:

> "They all followed him?" I asked, "Just like that?"
> "Of course. They would have followed him any-where."
> "I don't understand that. I didn't know a rabbi had that kind of power."
> "He's more than just a rabbi," Danny said. "He's a tzaddik [a venerated righteous man]."

All leaders require trust as a basis for their legitimacy and as the mortar that binds leader to follower. There can be no trust unless you, as a leader, act dependably and credibly, so that all your actions are consistent both with your stated intentions and with high moral standards. High moral standards are the key to creating an enduring sense of purpose that can earn long-term legitimacy and gain the endorsement of your followers.

You can establish a high moral standard in several ways. One is to demonstrate by your own behavior a commitment to the set of ethics you seek to institutionalize. You are the role model, so there must be as little a gap as possible between your public self and private self, as Peter Drucker reminds us so well:

> Leaders are expected to set an example. They are not supposed to behave as we know we behave. They are supposed to behave as we know that we ought to behave. . . .
> What executives do, what they believe and value,

what they reward and whom, are watched, seen, and
minutely interpreted throughout the whole organization. And nothing is noticed more quickly—and considered more significant—than a discrepancy between
what executives preach and what they expect their
associates to practice.

The Japanese recognize that there are really only
two demands of leadership: One is to accept that rank
does not confer privileges; it entails responsibilities.
The other is to acknowledge that leaders in an organization need to impose upon themselves that congru-
ence between words and deeds, between behavior and
professed beliefs and values, that we call personal
integrity.

As part of absorbing your moral principles into all you
do, you should take particular care in choosing whom to
hire, promote, and surround yourself with, particularly
your closest advisers. You can also establish the moral tone
of your organization in the way you articulate its sense of
purpose, in the reinforcement your principles receive from
outside the organization, and in the consonance of those
principles with the personal values of your employees and
those who deal with them.

Several studies reveal how leaders can miss the mark in
this area. When some 220 Pittsburgh-area managers were
asked to rank the values and attributes *they* most admired,
the top three values were self-respect, family security, and
freedom. The top three attributes were honesty, responsibility, and capability. Yet in another study of 202 *company*
codes of conduct, these characteristics were scarcely mentioned. Most of the company concerns were legalistic, cover-
ing matters such as relations with the U.S. government,
customers and suppliers, conflicts of interest, and political
contributions. In a third study of 6,000 executives and
middle managers, more than 70 percent said they felt pressure to conform to organizational standards and often com-

promised their personal principles to do so. Is it any surprise, then, that corporate leaders lose the trust of their followers and the public?

There is no room for this kind of compromise in futures-creative leadership. The first step in taking the high moral ground is to develop an attainable set of ethical principles worthy of commitment, consistent with high aspirations and suitable for the new age. While these principles will be somewhat different for each organization, at least four areas of personal responsibility are imperative in the new age of leadership, as follows:

1. Preventing or correcting the adverse impacts of organizational actions on society. Once it was said that "what's good for General Motors is good for the nation." Now the reverse is true. It is becoming vital for leaders to act so as to convey the unmistakable conviction that "what's good for society is good for us." This includes all organizational effects, whether environmental, political, social, aesthetic, or community. For example, upon learning that the odometers on some Chrysler cars had been disconnected during use by corporate executives, Lee Iacocca quickly admitted the error, accepted the responsibility, changed the practice, and compensated customers who had been misled. Similarly, leaders at Quaker Oats, Levi Strauss, Lincoln Electric, and some other firms insist on standards of testing far above those required by the government to prevent even the possibility of public harm from their products.

2. Commitment to the dignity of every individual—especially employees. It is no longer adequate to treat employees as "human resources," with concern only for their labor and not their lives. The organization hires a *whole* person, a person with needs as well as skills; head and heart as well as hands; a life to live as well as a livelihood to earn. What you do as a leader profoundly affects people's health, lifestyles, and sense of personhood. No leader will be able to create a viable future for an organization that does not respect the dignity of workers, customers, suppliers, and others who come into contact with it.

3. Creating fair and balanced communities of interest around important issues. With growing interdependence at every level, from the individual to the multinational, few things of importance can be done alone. As a futures-creative leader, you face the moral obligation to seek collaboration with other interested parties, to be open and truthful in dealing with them, and to treat them fairly even when they are less powerful (e.g., aged, poor, handicapped). To earn trust, you must make it absolutely clear that your "need to win" does not mean unconcern for who might be hurt in the process.

4. Seeing that the organization observes not only the letter but the intent of all laws that apply. When laws are passed, a clear signal is given that the community has unfulfilled needs, either to remedy current ills or to facilitate future social purposes. Your duty, then, is not only to see that the organization conforms to the letter of the law but also that it understands and respects the purpose and spirit behind it and the community interests being served. Any leader who allows the organization to skirt the edge of the law not only undermines its conscience and sense of good citizenship but may be creating circumstances that will give birth to new and more restrictive regulations in the future.

This is not an abstract set of principles to be enshrined in an organizational "code of ethics" and then forgotten. These principles must be real, apparent in everything you do and say and consistent with what actually happens from day to day.

Your acceptance of these personal responsibilities will mean resonance with those inside and outside the organization who are working for a better tomorrow. This kind of leadership will foster a working environment in which people can feel proud of their affiliation and uncompromised by their commitment. And you will sleep easier having, as Shakespeare said, "a peace above all earthly dignities, a still and quiet conscience."

DEVELOPING VISION

It is easy to recognize an organization led by an individual without vision. You find a confusing blur of intentions, people moving here and there, doing this and that, all seeming to have purpose but adding up to—what? When a futures-creative leader offers a convincing vision of the future, it is as if one had been looking at a fuzzy image through a camera lens, twisted the lens, and suddenly all comes into focus. But how does one become farsighted?

To be a futures-creative leader, you must learn to project your mind beyond the constraints of the present to seek signals from the future. Like a traveler gazing at a vibrant sunrise that promises a splendid new day, you seek out distant images that portend new possibilities for your organization. You are on a journey of discovery, a journey not dissimilar to the one described in this passage:

> The truth, as everyone knew, was that Davin . . . had not gone to Baghdad with Charlemagne's diplomatic mission. His friend Isaac the Radhanite had taken part in the expedition and told him about it when he returned. Davin had always regretted not having gone with him, and now that he was old he told the story of the journey to Baghdad over and over again. Perhaps by now he really believed he had gone there with Isaac. A dream of a cake is a dream, not a cake, but a dream of a journey is itself a kind of journey.

You need not necessarily set out on this journey alone. Often it is wise to draw from the organization, perhaps at a series of brainstorming sessions or a carefully planned retreat such as a QUEST exercise (see Appendix). During this journey of discovery, you are searching for clues to a puzzle. Some of the clues might be discovered as answers to questions such as the following:

- Which individuals and institutions have a stake in the future of this organization, and what are they trying to make happen?
- What could happen if we continue on our present path without any changes?
- What early warning signals might we detect if the external environment were to change substantially?
- What future events could happen, both inside and outside our organization, that would have a big impact on us, and how likely are they to occur?
- How much leverage do we have to influence the course of events, and how could that leverage be applied?
- What options could be available to us, and what might their consequences be?
- What future resources might be available, and what would we have to do to secure them?
- Of the alternative futures that might occur for our organization and its environments, which are more likely to be favorable to our survival and success?

Through a series of clues such as these, patterns may appear that suggest viable alternative images of the future. It then remains to articulate a vision out of these images. This challenges your imagination and creativity, to be sure, but also you are competing for mind space in the psyche of your organization. A persuasive vision ideally should provide a glimpse of something that everyone in the organization really "knew" was there but had never seen clearly before. It should provide a shock of recognition that has the power and intensity to command attention, evoking resonating images in the receiver—"I knew that. He sees it as I do."

How can you do this? Try to make the vision relate to something familiar in the organizational culture. Be sure that it is credible and easily understood, optimistic, and ennobling. Remind people of the tough things that need doing and the reasons for them. Elevate their aspirations. Show them a brighter, more successful future for themselves if the organization achieves its vision. In the end, your vision must provide the spark that ignites their energies and empowers them to move forward together with you toward a shared purpose.

LEADERSHIP INFORMATION SYSTEMS

Literally billions of dollars are spent today on management information systems. All kinds of systems and a great variety of applications are available, but no one seems to have thought to design an information system for the leader. It is not lack of information that concerns the leader; on the contrary, there is far too much, as we discovered earlier. Edna St. Vincent Millay may just as well have been thinking about leadership when she wrote:

Upon this gifted age, in its dark hour,
Rains from the sky a meteoric shower
Of facts . . . they lie unquestioned, uncombined.
Wisdom enough to leech us of our ill
Is daily spun; but there exists no loom
To weave it into fabric; . . .

The most useful information to you as a futures-creative leader would enhance development of the seven megaskills identified earlier. For example, farsightedness could be enhanced with information that contributes to, or changes, your images of the future. Similarly, information that tracks your organization's ethical practices, projects where the organization is headed, or reveals the expectations of key constituencies, could be of great use to you if suitably captured and interpreted. Although it would be beyond the scope of this book to design such a system, it would not be out of place to suggest a few of its critical components in the following sections.

Trend Monitoring

The most valuable information to support farsightedness appears in trends, patterns of movement of data series over time that, if continued, suggest potential opportunities, vulnerabilities, or threats for the organization. Much of this information, including demographic information, long-term political trends, projections of ecological changes over time, technological forecasts, and analyses of shifts in social values, is readily available. In addition, there is a plethora of think tanks, trade associations, professional journals, government agencies, university research centers, and con-sultants dedicated to the production and dissemination of trend information. Finally, an endless stream of less formal trend data is available through colleagues, board members, friends, and associates.

Much of this information, obtainable at low cost, is doubtless already available in your organization. The prob-lem is that it often reaches the organization in a disorga-nized and fragmentary fashion; some may be of doubtful credibility. The people who receive or collect the data may fail to recognize the data's relevance, so that important ideas are filtered out unintentionally. And rarely is the information brought to the attention of leaders in a timely and useful manner.

Thus a cornerstone of a leadership information system would be a trend monitoring system designed to sense, collect, interpret, and present trend pattern data about internal and external environments. This knowledge could enhance your farsightedness or alter an existing image of the future of the organization.

Conceptually, at least, designing such a system would not be too difficult. Simply draw a matrix with the major environments of interest across the top and the major product lines, customer sets, and resources down the side, as illustrated in Figure 7 for a hypothetical oil company. A rudimentary trend monitoring system could then be established simply by assigning cells in the matrix to individuals in the organization for monitoring. For example, one cell might be concerned with the future legal/regulatory climate for petrochemicals; it would monitor all relevant health and safety standards, state and local zoning restrictions, environmental regulations, judicial opinions on product liability, and the like. Those whose task it is to monitor this area would be sent all relevant information received by the organization. In time they would become experts, able to produce forecasts as needed. They might issue memos or conduct briefings for leaders at various levels in the organization, suggesting where the trends are heading or what implications they may have for current visions of the organization's future.

Some large corporations have already established so-called issues management staffs for trend monitoring and for providing early warning of emerging issues for their top management. Although often concentrating on issues only a few years into the future, such staffs are able to detect weak signals of longer term issues that would be of particular interest to futures-creative leaders.

Use of Experts

Another part of a leadership information system would be the use of experts to provide forecasts or to judge the timing, likelihood, and implications of possible developments that can shape the future environment of the organization. The QUEST approach shows one way you could collect structured expert opinion from knowledgeable people inside the organization. The well-known Delphi technique and other questionnaire and interview processes can readily be used with outside experts. Polls and surveys offer still another way to collect judgments relevant to the future

FIGURE 7: TREND MONITORING STRUCTURE FOR A
HYPOTHETICAL OIL COMPANY

	Economic	Sociocultural	Legal/Regulatory	Technological	Industrial
Product Lines					
Vehicle fuels					
Lubricants					
Heating oil					
Petrochemicals					
Customer Sets					
Industrial firms					
Gasoline distributors					
Government users					
Power stations					
Other					
Resources					
Domestic oil					
Foreign oil					
Capital markets					
Labor markets					
Refineries					
Distribution system					

ENVIRONMENTS

when other information is not available or is suspect.

Stakeholder Intelligence Systems

As a futures-creative leader, you should be particularly interested in the future directions, ambitions, and prospects of major stakeholders in your organization. Competitor intelligence systems already exist in many firms, particularly in Japan and Korea, and in certain American industries. These are not cloak-and-dagger spy operations; rather, they are attempts to understand what might happen next by collecting publicly available information at trade meetings and technical conferences; reviewing patent applications and government filings; studying reports of investment analysts; and monitoring new product introductions and trade fairs. For example, IBM-watching has evolved into a high art in the computer industry, and many consultants make a fine living doing so.

Of course, customers and clients are probably the most watched constituency. The entire marketing research industry is devoted to a search for patterns of consumer usage and the evolution of new tastes or expectations. Any leadership information system would have to be adept at picking up early warning of new market needs or the decline of current consumer preferences. Much grief at Warner Communications could have been avoided, for example, had its Atari subsidiary been able to position itself for the precipitous decline in demand for its electronic games.

Other stakeholders may be of considerable long-run interest. Lobbyists are often deputized to report on the prospects for new legislation. Political campaigns, party platforms, and government appointments are also closely watched for clues to policy changes. Information may be needed on the plans of raw materials suppliers. All these and more belong in the leadership information system.

Ethical Compliance

Because the moral climate of the organization is so important for your maintenance of trust, an information system can help by tracking and reporting trends in compliance with your standards. Examples of useful data would be changes in the number of customer and employee complaints or lawsuits around issues of fairness. The trend in union grievances, in whistle-blowing incidents, and in reported cases of petty theft or vandalism can also provide clues to the moral tone of the organization. Exit interviews are another source of information. Opinion polls reporting public views of your organization's reputation also may help to measure what Washington pundits call the sleaze factor.

These examples suggest how you could build a leadership information system that would support all the megaskills, especially those concerned with farsightedness, learning, managing interdependence, and designing systems. In the end, of course, it is what you *do* with the information that counts. When it comes to using the information for making things happen, a futures-creative leader must choose actions that are appropriate not just for now but for the longer term future. Strategies, in other words, must be robust.

DESIGNING ROBUST STRATEGIES

A strategy is a course of purposeful actions designed to move an organization in an intended direction. Some strategies may be handled as part of the management function, such as a strategy for expanding plant capacity or launching a new advertising campaign. However, there are strategic issues that must command your attention as a leader, and for which you have sole responsibility. These issues have the following properties:

• They are concerned with long-term matters, usually five years or more.

• They affect the way the organization conducts its business in a fundamental and enduring manner.

- They affect the entire organization, or at least many functions or divisions.

- They affect the performance of the organization in a vital way. Indeed, if there is no action, or if the action is untimely or inappropriate, the organization's very existence may be threatened.

For a corporation, some issues that would fit these criteria would be whether to enter a new line of business or close an existing one; whether to open an operation in a foreign country; how to respond to the possibility of severe new environmental restrictions; or what to do about a technological breakthrough by a competitor. For a government agency, strategic issues facing the leader might be how to serve a new constituency; whether to embark on a long-term collaboration with agencies at other levels (e.g., joint power arrangements); or how fast procedures should be automated. Other organizations face similar issues.

When a leader is faced with choosing a strategy, the typical approach is to establish a set of assumptions about the future and then to select the option that promises to work best under those circumstances. If the decision is about a new line of business, for example, assumptions are developed on market potential, competitive strength, new venture costs, and reasonable expectation of profits. If the venture advances in the firm's intended direction and promises an adequate return, then the decision is made to go ahead.

For the futures-creative leader, however, this procedure is not good enough. It is as if a bet is being placed about how the future will evolve. If assumptions prove to be correct, the bet is won and the payoff is as expected; if not, the bet is lost. If the situation is salvageable, additional costs are incurred to cope with the unexpected circumstances, and the payoff may be diminished or even turned into a loss. Many leaders seem comfortable with this strategy—especially if they can limit their losses if the gamble turns out to be a losing one. But it does put the organization needlessly at risk.

The problem is that the betting procedure does not acknowledge uncertainty. The temptation is always strong to describe the future in terms of an extended present as if the experience of the past decade is simply to be extrapolated into a sort of "muddling through" scenario. Even sophisticated financial analysts may couch assumptions in terms of expected value—i.e., multiplying costs and payoffs by the probabilities of their occurrence. In either case you would end up with a single set of assumptions for a future that is inherently unpredictable. This virtually guarantees surprise.

There is something better than a betting procedure. As a futures-creative leader, you can seek *robust* strategies that are designed to yield satisfactory payoffs under *all* possible scenarios. To do this, you need not a singular forecast but a deep understanding of the range of possibilities that can occur. Often these are embodied in scenarios of the future that describe what can happen under widely differing sets of assumptions. For example, one scenario might imagine world peace; another, a major economic depression; a third, a more open and thriving international trading system; and so on.

Such scenarios are useful in many ways. They help clarify how changes may interact over time. They make it easier to evaluate the consequences of choices, as well as their favorable and unfavorable outcomes and their exposure to threats. They force consideration of issues and options that otherwise might go overlooked. They reduce the domain of surprise and facilitate quick reaction to changes because they have been fully rehearsed in the mind.

With the full range of scenarios in hand, you can develop a robust strategy in two ways. One is by hedging, as in a diversification strategy. By not putting all your eggs in one basket but spreading them around, high payoffs on one investment can offset losses in others. Another hedging strategy is sharing the risk with others, as farmers do when they sell futures contracts to lock in certain returns for themselves while letting others take profits or losses on price fluctuations. A hedging strategy will not have as high a payoff as the betting strategy when the assumptions about the future turn out to be correct, but it will do better in most other cases.

Robustness can also be achieved by investing in flexibility so that the organization can respond to a range of circumstances as they occur. An example would be an electric utility deliberately designing its boilers to burn a variety of fuels, from oil and gas to coal slurries and garbage. It costs to build in flexibility, of course, but the payoff comes when the world changes in unexpected ways and the organization is positioned to take advantage of them.

Scenarios of the future lead to flexibility because they help you see how much lead time you might have in which to react under varying circumstances. They also help you determine which actions could be taken now to speed up response times and lower costs later. By reducing the domain of surprise and anticipating what reactions would be appropriate, you can design flexibility into the organization. In addition, if there is a trend monitoring system, you will be able to build in the kind of flexibility that enables survival even under adverse circumstances.

Robust strategies, whether hedging or flexibility, are becoming much more important in the new age of leadership. Begin right now to examine your existing strategies to determine how likely it is that they would succeed if conditions were to change substantially. For change they will, and the measure of your success as a leader will be how well prepared you and your organization are to meet the new challenges. It will no longer be acceptable merely to shrug, as many leaders now do, saying, "We didn't expect that to happen [e.g., oil shortage, radiation leak, new auto emission standards, tough foreign competition, etc.]; nobody did, so we're not responsible." Society and shareholders will respond, "Yes, you are. That's what we pay you for, to be ready for change. If you aren't responsible for the future of your own organization, who is?"

PERSONAL DEVELOPMENT

The new age of leadership demands leaders who are forever renewing and reinventing themselves. They are expected to be lifelong learners, driven by dreams, opportunities, and challenges always to *be* more so that they can *do* more. How, then, to develop your own skills? Here are ten suggestions:

1. Seek leadership responsibilities early and often. Deliberately seek leadership positions at every stage of your life. If you're employed but not yet in a leadership position, volunteer to coach a football team or head a Boy Scout troop. Start a small business or take charge of local activities in a political campaign. Offer to head committees in your church or local community. You will learn a great deal about leadership from each of these experiences, regardless of outcome. As you develop a track record for making things happen, you will come to see yourself as a leader and have others recognize your leadership abilities.

2. Find a mentor or role model. Successful leaders often point to an individual who was instrumental in their own development. Find an admired leader in your organization or someone elsewhere who has earned respect for his or her accomplishments. You may find a role model in historical figures, as Martin Luther King did in Mahatma Gandhi or as John F. Kennedy did in writing about great American leaders in his book *Profiles in Courage.* The role of the mentor is not to produce a clone, for circumstances in the future will surely be different from those under which the mentor achieved success. It is, rather, to impart a way of thinking and acting, a philosophy of life, and some encouragement when things don't seem to be working out. After you have had some successful leadership experiences, try to be a mentor to others, for there is much to be learned in teaching what you know. In becoming the role model, in helping others learn from their own mistakes, and in encouraging long-range thinking, you will be reinventing yourself while at the same time designing the future of your organization.

3. Develop farsightedness. Train yourself to think through the consequences of current trends and potential future developments. Read widely to learn what experts in economics, politics, sociology, and technology think is likely to happen. Seek forecasts from colleagues and important constituencies. Be sure to avoid expediency; concentrate your attention and actions on longer range concerns. Work with others to test your ideas about the future and to develop and communicate a sense of vision.

4. Master the skills of interdependence. A leader is like the king on the chessboard, weak and exposed without the support of others with different abilities. Learn how to make others feel good about themselves, about the organization they are a part of, and about their prospects for personal growth. Learn how to select and motivate people, how to pay attention to their concerns, and how to inspire them to accept responsibility for the organization's future. Learn how to promote cooperation and teamwork, how to form coalitions and joint ventures, and how to achieve unanimity. Although a large body of useful literature on interpersonal relations is available and can provide valuable insights, these skills are best developed through experience.

5. Become a "world citizen." As the United States becomes more concerned with international issues and organizations find their boundaries stretched overseas, it becomes advantageous for leaders to demonstrate their proficiency in this area. Learning languages, seeking opportunities to serve overseas, studying foreign literature and cultures, traveling, and having friends from other countries are all useful ways to broaden your perspective and become "international-ized."

6. *Develop personal character, integrity, and trust.* As stated earlier, futures-creative leaders need to take the high road. The only way to do this is to set high personal standards and to comport yourself so that no question about your integrity arises. Ask yourself a series of questions before acting: Who would be helped by your actions and who would be hurt? Are you proud of your decisions and of the intentions they embody? Could they be misunderstood? Would you have the slightest hesitation if your actions were to be reported in the morning news or if you were asked to defend them on a talk show? Would an alternative action achieve the same ends for the organization but be more socially responsible? Such tests can help you develop a personal code of behavior that when consistently and de-pendably applied will create confidence and trust in your integrity.

7. *Seek varied job assignments.* Develop a deep understand-ing of how your organization works, what the crucial deci-sions are, and how they affect outside constituencies. As part of your personal development, seek opportunities to start something from scratch or rescue an ailing department. Join a staff function, such as planning or marketing re-search, to gain broader perspectives. Work with other lead-ers in task forces addressed to critical strategic issues. For the most part you will have to seek these opportunities out, because American organizations tend to move people around in job assignments to suit the organization and not as part of a systematic plan for developing leaders.

8. *Think like a researcher.* Develop your natural sense of curiosity and creativity so that complex and ambiguous situations become challenges rather than stumbling blocks. Be willing to experiment and take risks. Read a lot, so that

you become skilled at organizing knowledge, separating what is important from what is not. Develop your ability to see relationships, build mental models of how the world works, and reason from inadequate data. Become skilled in communicating what you have learned, orally and in written form, so that others will not misinterpret your views.

9. Design your leadership job carefully. Most leaders design their own jobs, a freedom that goes with the territory and one of the things leaders like most about their positions. But take care to concentrate your efforts only on a few matters of the highest long-term priority. Jimmy Carter had problems with this and became enmeshed in the details of so many different issues that he was unable to project a coherent vision or set of priorities.

Resist the temptation to spread yourself too thin, especially as lower level leaders and managers seek your views and guidance on their problems. Instead, appoint good people to head operational departments and encourage them to make decisions and take risks on their own. Surround yourself with intelligent, energetic aides and deputies who can handle many of the nonstrategic matters that will reach your desk. Finally, develop a personal philosophy to guide the exercise of your leadership responsibilities. Figure 8 is an example of such a set of principles derived from the earlier discussion of futures-creative leadership.

10. Have fun at what you do. All this is serious business, of course, but not *just* serious business. Leaders should, and do, also have fun doing their jobs. And why not? You will get to work on important issues, have freedom to be creative, enjoy latitude in designing your own job. You will be in a position to really make a difference. You will earn the respect of other people and may be seen as a pillar of your community. Chances are you will be paid pretty well, too. If all that doesn't sound like a formula for self-fulfillment, then the term has lost its meaning. Science fiction writer

**FIGURE 8: AN EXAMPLE OF A PERSONAL PHILOSOPHY
FOR THE FUTURES-CREATIVE LEADER**

1. I believe in progress—that is, that my organization will perform better and make more valuable contributions tomorrow
than it does today. I am optimistic about our prospects and
regard it as my duty to provide a vision that will energize
and inspire people and guide their decisions toward a
brighter future.

2. The managers in my organization are responsible for today's performance, and I will do what I can to help them.
However, I readily accept my responsibility for the future of
the organization and will avoid the temptation to achieve
short-term gains at the expense of long-term viability.

3. I can never know the future because I do not believe it to
be predestined and because what I and others do can make
a difference in the outcome. However, I can and must make
every effort to understand the forces that together are
shaping the future and the role my organization can play
relative to these forces. I view this understanding as the beginning of wisdom, without which leadership cannot and
should not be exercised.

4. I believe there are alternative futures and many paths my
organization can follow, only one of which is to continue on
its present course. My job is to select a direction and speed
for my organization so that it can succeed in a wide range
of possible external environments. I must also keep the organization's attention focused on this direction so that there
is a shared context within which to interpret changes.

5. I will be open to new ideas and will lead the search for the
right issues to address—i.e., those that matter most to the
future of my organization. Because others will be influenced
strongly by what I proclaim to be important, feasible, worthwhile, or necessary, I will offer these judgments only after
careful reflection on the consequences for all those who
have a stake in our future. Also, I will not shrink from articulating these assumptions so that they can be examined and
discussed, and I will make it safe—in fact desirable—for critics to express their reservations about them.

6. Because I believe in anticipative management, I will recognize, respect, and reward futures-creative thinking, and I will
embrace experimentation and innovation within the
organization.

Ray Bradbury offered the following advice for business leaders:

> If your meeting room, your board room, or your office (take your pick) isn't a nursery for ideas, a rumpus room where seals frolic, forget it. Burn the table, lock the room, fire the clerks. You will rarely come up with any ideas worth entertaining. The dull room with the heavy people trudging in with long faces to solve problems by beating them to death is very death itself. Serious confrontations rarely arrive at serious ends. Unless the people you meet with are funloving kids out for a romp, tossing ideas like confetti, and letting the damn bits fall where they may, no spirit will ever rouse, no notion will ever birth, no love will be mentioned, no climax reached. You must swim at your meetings, you must jump for baskets, you must take hefty swings for great or missed drives, you must run and dive, you must fall and roll, and when the fun stops, get the hell out.

Taken seriously and acted on, these suggestions can help you develop the capacity to become a futures-creative leader. Now let's turn our attention to what it will take for your organization to become a leader in the twenty-first century.

9

BUILDING ORGANIZATIONAL CAPITAL

"We are made wise not by the recollections of our past but by the responsibility for our future."

—George Bernard Shaw

ORGANIZATIONS PROVIDE THE warp and the woof of modern society. Nearly all of our work is done in organizations, and most transactions take place with or between them. Just as an individual can be a leader in an organization, so can an organization be a leader in its field. A corporation can lead its industry, setting the terms of competition, pacing innovation, pointing the way toward the next level of performance. A hospital, union, government agency, baseball team, or museum similarly can lead its peer institutions, becoming the one that all the others measure themselves against.

There seems to be a natural tendency to want to be the best, and there are real benefits in doing so. Corporations with the leading market share usually are the most profitable. The best private universities and museums attract the most donations. Not only do resources tend to flow to the leading organizations, but so do noneconomic benefits such as recognition, status, and legitimacy. The most talented people also tend to be attracted to the leading organizations.

In short, success breeds success among organizations as well as among people. Organizations, like people, are born, experience growth pains, and go through various stages of maturity. They learn and adapt to change; operate within social constraints, laws, and codes of acceptable behavior; and develop a personality and reputation in their dealings with others. Their success is measured in both economic and psychosocial terms.

Because organizations share these characteristics with individuals, it should be possible for us to learn how they can assume leadership among their peers by reviewing the seven megaskills in organizational terms. In fact, as we shall see shortly, this is a very useful perspective, for the futures-creative aspects of organizational leadership have not been sufficiently recognized.

FARSIGHTEDNESS: THE FUTURE-ORIENTED ORGANIZATION

Organizations, like people, tend to be dominated by a particular time perspective. Some are dominated by their *past*, as the glory of earlier successes give birth to rituals, myths, and traditions that are designed to perpetuate the formula for success. Military organizations often are dominated by past glories, which may be why they are more able to fight the last war than the next one. Walt Disney was such a compelling leader that it took many years after his death for his corporation to stop asking what Walt would have done every time a new opportunity or problem was encountered. General Motors and Polaroid are other examples of corporations that have found it difficult to break with their pasts. This is also true of most churches, museums, and orchestras—which, after all, are designed to preserve the past, as are some cities and communities (Venice, for example).

Even more of a problem for modern society, however, is the *present*-orientedness of many organizations for which that position is no longer appropriate. The present is simply *too present*—and for many reasons:

1. Pressure for short-term results is immense. In the private sector, if for even one or two quarters earnings do not meet expectations, Wall Street becomes apoplectic. Demand for the firm's stock declines, loans become more difficult to obtain, and corporate raiders begin circling like sharks. The typical response is to implement crash programs to cut costs, increase profits, and drive up the price of the stock. The easiest way to do this is to cut functions that show up as short-term costs but whose benefits are not currently visible—plant maintenance, research and development, strategic planning, etc.

The situation is no different in the public sector, where elected officials have at most two to four years to prove themselves or be displaced by another administration. Indeed, there is nothing a public official likes so much as a well-publicized short-term gain, for this is the currency that buys power and career advancement. Knowing that the electorate is impatient for results, the official avidly studies opinion polls to learn which results can be converted quickly into votes. Short-term demands often seem to drive out long-term considerations, even for well-intentioned public administrators.

2. The full weight of management theory and practice, as developed over the past few decades, has been applied to making decision-making processes in organizations more present-oriented. A high value is placed on collecting and analyzing data on recent performance. Models are built to replicate past experience so that "optimal" decisions can be taken. Behavioral science is employed to measure stakeholder preferences, consumer tastes, and worker attitudes. These techniques are doubtlessly valuable, but they force attention on the present and recent past, which can be measured and analyzed, at the expense of the future, which can't. It is as if the professionals believe that the best driver must be the one who has the clearest rear-view mirror.

3. Organizations frequently are designed for stability and control instead of adaptability and change. Despite nearly universal condemnation by management scholars and the general public, the slow and ponderous bureaucratic form of organization persists throughout business and government. Although new products are introduced with increasing rapidity, most tend to be small improvements on existing products so that production systems need not be disrupted—e.g., a new fender for an automobile or a new lens for a camera. Radical innovations—the electric automobile or the instant-developing camera—seem to require totally new companies or even industries. Similarly, major government initiatives seem to spawn new organizations, since the old ones are already busy and often do not contain the flexibility to adapt to new needs.

4. In many organizations, no one seems to be in charge of the future, whereas responsibilities are clearly assigned and jurisdictions well staked out for current operations. Sometimes a planning staff is formed to deal with long-range problems, but even then many planning staffs spend a great deal of time on problems of operational planning—budgeting, scheduling, and the like. This type of planning is largely designed to perpetuate the present rather than to create a new future.

The present-oriented organization is appropriate only where routine and efficiency are of critical importance, where the external environment is relatively well understood and changing at a slow or controllable pace, and where there are sufficiently long reaction times to deal with major changes. This describes few of today's situations—and even fewer of tomorrow's.

If an organization's decisions are based on premises that may shortly be proved false, or if the "mean time between surprises" is decreasing, present-oriented decisions are not likely to be effective and may have serious long-term consequences. If the environment is complex and uncertain, rigid organizational structures are precisely the opposite of what is required. If the environment is changing in unpredictable directions, then planning to perpetuate the present constitutes an unnecessary and even dangerous limitation on the sources of new opportunity. These are the very conditions we are now experiencing, so it is becoming much less likely that a present-oriented organization can lead its industry or peer group. In order to lead, organizations must become more future-oriented. Making them so is a major leadership responsibility of our age.

A *future-oriented* organization is defined as one that takes responsibility for creating its own future when possible and adapting to change when necessary, through a continuous process of anticipation, adaptation, and change. Some examples of future-oriented organizations are IBM, Merck, and Shell Oil in the private sector, and America's NASA, Japan's MITI, and the European Common Market in the public sector.

The future-oriented organization tends to be driven by forecasts rather than current problems. It values preventive over curative action. Such an organization is constantly in the process of becoming what it wishes to be—in sharp contrast to the present-oriented organization in which the long-run shape of the organization is determined by a series of short-run decisions that seldom accumulate to a desirable end.

The leadership of a future-oriented organization uses anticipation of the future as its pacing mechanism. As a result, lead time becomes one of the most important resources to be managed, and organizational processes and structures are designed for the effective use of lead time. As an army unit posts sentries so does a business look for emerging issues, a political party take preference polls, and a school system watch the demographics, each to get some early warning of impending changes.

The future-oriented organization places high value on active anticipation and systematic design of the organization's future, not reaction to changes that have already occurred. By squarely facing the fact that decisions taken today constrain and influence the future and that such decisions cannot be avoided, leaders in such organizations lengthen their time horizons and broaden their search for opportunities.

But how far into the future should attention be directed? Two time horizons affect this decision. One is the *commitment time*, the time over which decisions can reasonably be made to allocate resources, design and implement programs, or complete an important transition (such as the introduction of a new product or the opening of a new facility). In most large organizations, commitment time is generally three to five years. In others, it can stretch to seven or more years, such as when an electric utility commits to the development of a new power plant. When organizations establish a long-range planning process, it usually covers this commitment time horizon.

The other type of time horizon might be called the *scanning time*, the time *beyond* the commitment time that the organization must understand if it is to make intelligent choices. Typically, this period is five to twenty years or more.

Thus commitment time is the time it takes to implement a major change while scanning time is the time it takes to realize the benefits of that change. If a steel manufacturer decides to build a new plant, it could take five years or more to complete site selection, gain zoning approvals, design the buildings and actually finish the construction. So far, the plant has had no impact on the firm's revenues. Now in the fifth year, it is ready to open and is expected to pay back its investment over the subsequent five to twenty years. The world will have changed significantly over this period. Regulations might differ, the technology could change, and new materials, say ceramics, might steal markets the plant was designed to serve. So if today's decision is to be a wise one, it must be taken in light of informed anticipation of circumstances five to twenty-five years hence, the scanning time horizon.

A future-oriented organization, therefore, is constantly scanning the distant horizon to learn what might work and how to proceed. By studying trends and possible developments, it hopes to anticipate threats and opportunities with sufficient lead time for appropriate action. Such an organization promotes broad participation in this search for useful images of the future, with great stress on creativity and the sharing of responsibility. To promote flexibility, people are encouraged to experiment and to take risks as part of the price of successful adaptation over the long term.

Thus organizations that aspire to leadership must move from being present-oriented to being future-oriented. The differences are profound, as suggested in Figure 9, and characterize the opposite of how many organizations have been behaving in the past few years. Goodyear Tire and Rubber, for example, cut their operating, plant investment, and research budgets to increase short-term profits, weakening themselves against the long-term challenge of foreign tire makers. In the name of becoming "lean and mean," many U.S. firms have cut the very heart out of their long-term ability to lead their industries.

MASTERY OF CHANGE: ORGANIZATIONAL CAPITAL

To be a leader among its peers, an organization must first

FIGURE 9: DIFFERENCES BETWEEN PRESENT- AND FUTURE-ORIENTED ORGANIZATIONS

	Present-Oriented	Future-Oriented
+Basis for Performance	Short-term results	Long-term results
+Primary Thrust	Efficiency	Effectiveness
+Organizational Structure	Relatively rigid	Relatively flexible
+Decision-Making Emphasis	Operational	Strategic
+Planning Mode	Reactive	Proactive
+Planning Stimulus	Problem-driven	Forecast-driven
+Constituencies Recognized	Few	Many
+Environmental Assumptions	Slow change	Rapid change

be strong itself. Organizations become strong by accumulating three kinds of capital. One is *physical wealth,* the total stock of assets accumulated to date, including buildings, inventories, cash, investments, and financial instruments. A second form is *human capital,* which consists of the cumulative experience, knowledge, managerial talent, information, and skills possessed by individuals in the organization.

Physical and human capital are well recognized by economists, but the third form, *organizational capital,* is not. To understand why organizational capital is so vital, we need to consider its components, as follows:

1. Reputation. Organizations build confidence and trust among their various constituencies, especially among customers or clients. Although intangible and hard to measure, an organization's reputation and image are so important that billions of dollars in advertising, public relations, and marketing research are invested each year to create and enhance favorable images.

For many organizations, such as Coca-Cola, Disney, the Red Cross, and any accounting firm, reputation is the most precious of assets, the source of their competitive edge and the foundation for their future growth. It is closely related to organizational integrity, which will be discussed later in this chapter.

2. Option Space. Organizations are constantly trying to increase the degrees of freedom they enjoy in their decision making. They do this by increasing their ability to respond to new challenges in various ways. They can expand and diversify their scope of operations, perhaps by adding new products or markets; build flexibility and adaptability into their operating processes; invest in research and development; or expand their capacity for anticipating change and thinking strategically. In all these examples, the organization has increased its ability to survive and thrive under uncertain future circumstances.

3. Supportive Cultures. Organizations become stronger as they build cohesive, mutually supportive social cultures. Teamwork is extremely important because it allows people to pool their skills and knowledge to solve problems and seek improvements. The Los Angeles Lakers are so formidable because the players have worked together for so long that they know precisely what each can contribute, and they each act unselfishly in seeking the team's success. Loyalty to each other and to the organization brings many benefits in terms of lower turnover, improved quality, and mutual trust. Many organizations invest huge sums in organizational development and training programs to achieve these benefits.

4. Leadership. High-quality leadership is a form of organizational capital, especially when it exists at all levels over a long period of time.

Thousands of books have been written about how to increase the physical capital of organizations, yet much less is written about human and organizational capital, which are more vital to organizational growth and leadership. For example, in World War II, the physical capital of Germany and Japan was largely destroyed, but these countries were completely rebuilt in a couple of decades because their human and organizational capital was largely intact. Compare their performance with that of, say, Mexico, which came out of the same war with its physical assets totally intact but with far less human and organizational capital. Savvy investors realize the superiority of human and organizational capital to physical capital, as shown in their willingness to pay much higher price-earnings ratios for firms like Microsoft and Disney than for firms proportionately richer in physical assets, such as General Motors or Mobil.

How is it possible to create organizational capital? Every organization serves some customer or client population. Satisfaction of client needs may be measured directly, as when a corporation plots growth in sales and market share, or indirectly, as when the postal service measures how much the system is used or universities measure the quality of their graduates. When an organization serves its clients well, it enhances its reputation and option space. In doing so, it also has many opportunities to build leadership and teamwork. In a real sense, organizational capital is both the product of a job well done and a measure of the organization's potential for providing additional services to its client community.

To illustrate the active pursuit of organizational capital, let's consider the Xerox Corporation. Once the undisputed world leader in photocopiers, Xerox lost market share and initiative to Japanese competitors in the early eighties. In a determined bid to recapture its leadership, Xerox set about aggressively to create organizational capital. In a top-to-bottom redesign of its corporate culture, the company put product quality and customer satisfaction above all else. All Xerox employees were given at least forty-eight hours of training in "Leadership Through Quality." Annual "Teamwork Days" were held to honor innovative employee teams and to celebrate joint efforts to improve products and service. Employees were urged to seek opportunities to improve the business and were generously rewarded for doing so. As a result, Xerox's reputation and market share have greatly improved, its option space has expanded, loyalty and teamwork have improved, and the company is once again optimistic about its long-term prospects.

Organizational capital can also be destroyed. When a corporate raider puts a firm "in play," the physical capital may be only minimally affected, but the human and organizational capital can be quickly dissipated. Option space is reduced by loading the firm up with debt. Teamwork is destroyed as jobs are threatened, and the workers' loyalty diminishes. Reputation and image decline as people who are less interested in quality and satisfied clients than in quick returns for so-called investors (who may, in fact, be little more than short-term speculators), are put in charge. Organizational capital can rarely survive a fire sale.

ORGANIZATION DESIGN: BUILDING DISTINCTIVE COMPETENCE

Organization design affects leadership both substantively and structurally. The substantive issue is how the organization designs its niche in the environment. The structural issue is how it matches its physical, human, and organizational resources to that niche.

In the natural world, every organism exists in an environment to which it is uniquely well suited. Through the process of evolution, each organism has come to occupy an ecological niche that defines its relationship to the environment and to all other organisms. A plant, for example, may exist only under certain specific conditions—i.e., temperature, rainfall, seasonality, sunshine, soil, and synergy with other living things that provide services such as pollination, fertilization, shade, and protection.

Human organizations share many characteristics with

natural organisms in this regard. They too must find an appropriate niche in their external environment within which to function and grow. Think of the unique niches carved out by Crown Books, the *Wall Street Journal*, or Santa Fe, New Mexico. Within the organization, specialization of functions exists as in any other organism, so that each unit deals only with as much of the environment as it can handle effectively—production, purchasing, recruiting, sales, etc. Abrupt environmental change can cause the death of an organization as easily as it can for any other organism that has insufficient lead time or resources to adapt. Bankruptcy courts are littered with examples.

For an organization to be a leader, it must first design its own niche; it must develop its *distinctive competence*, the job or service it can do better than anyone else. For example, a piano manufacturer like Steinway may become a leader by choosing to produce only the highest quality instruments. A competing piano manufacturer may stake out a leadership position in another part of the market, perhaps emphasizing high-technology production coupled with low-cost assembly. Atlantic Richfield found its distinctive competence in low-cost, no-frills gasoline stations coupled with mini-markets. The same principle applies in every field. Some architectural firms have created specialized niches for themselves—airport design, schools, bank buildings. Some farmers have found their distinctive competence in raising exotic fruits, pesticide-free tomatoes, or low-fat beef. Cities have tried to differentiate themselves by being known as an international city (e.g., Geneva); a conservator city (e.g., Venice); a regional center (e.g., Dallas/Fort Worth); a recreational center (e.g., Aspen); a commercial city (e.g., London), and so on. Because no organization can be all things to all people in an era of complexity and change, it is incumbent on would-be leader organizations to seek out their distinctive competence.

Developing a distinctive competence is not as difficult as it may seem at first glance. It is always possible to find a niche at the very-high-quality end of a product or service spectrum (e.g., the very finest knives, shoes, or word processing software, etc.) or at the lowest cost end (e.g., the least expensive radio, electric shaver, or tax preparation service, etc.). Unique features or services can always be added to a product or service to differentiate it (e.g., the longest warranty period, the best design, the fewest calories, etc.). For others, a patent position, a geographic location, a packaging innovation, or a unique mode of service delivery may provide a distinctive competence. One company listed all the technologies in which it was proficient and then deliberately created products that required combinations of their technologies. Competitors could rarely match them because they were always deficient in one or another technological capability.

The other major design question involves structure. Most large organizations have been moving toward flatter, looser, more decentralized flexible organizations. The idea is to retain the advantages of large size—strong financial position, synergies among units, global presence, market strength, etc.—while still reducing red tape and moving decision making closer to the customer. The leading edge organizations, those that have moved closest toward adapting to rapid change and frequent innovation, have already adopted a sort of hybrid large/small form. For example:

▷ Johnson & Johnson, with $8 billion in global sales of health care products, is organized into 165 largely autonomous units, some with less than 100 employees and others with as many as 5,000. Each unit has a well-defined and self-contained market, allowing it to move with the agility of a small entrepreneur in response to market shifts, and yet benefit from the reputation and financial power of its parent. Apart from its high profitability and growth, this structure gives Johnson & Johnson a remarkable ability to develop and test leaders throughout the organization.

▷ General Electric, while not as decentralized as Johnson &

Johnson, also has tried to create a hybrid large/small organization by cutting layers of management, flattening the organization, and giving lower level managers enough authority and responsibility to allow them to experience a sense of ownership of their unit.

▷Colgate Palmolive, General Foods, and Scott Paper, among others, have retained their large organizations but established internal venture capital operations designed to create "intrapreneurs." In this way, people are empowered to act boldly and take risks that would not be acceptable in the parent bureaucracy. They operate outside the traditional corporate culture but can draw on the reputation and financial resources of the parent.

In each of these cases, a large company has found a way to allow each of its units to develop its own distinctive competence and to concentrate on its own niche. In doing so, each unit can operate at an appropriate scale in terms of market size, technology, and geographic distribution. These firms have also multiplied the opportunities for leadership experiences internally and have created portfolios of businesses that balance risk and opportunity. Finally, this approach leaves top executives free to concentrate on long-term issues associated with the growing organization.

ANTICIPATORY LEARNING: THE STRATEGY PROCESS

Organizations learn constantly, just as people do. When an organization takes an action, it gets feedback at many levels, which may alter its behavior the next time. Some learning happens deliberately, as when an organization adjusts to a major reorganization or when formal training courses are conducted. Other learning is less intentional, as when an organization is surprised by a technological breakthrough or a change in government regulations. But if the purpose is anticipatory learning, there is nothing so powerful as an effective strategy process. By strategy process, I mean the way an organization establishes its objectives, defines its strategic options, decides on a plan of action, and implements it. The strategy process *need* not be formalized to be effective, but if an organization aspires to be future-oriented, here are some reasons for establishing an orderly, continuous, and systematic strategy process:

▷Strategy processes can serve as a coordinative mechanism for the leader by requiring the articulation of forecasts and assumptions and the formulation of programs involving many units of the organization. By involving all levels of management, strategy formulation can lead to a sharing of values, purpose, and direction. The strategy process also serves as a useful framework for resource allocation by assuring that budgets reflect long-term considerations and that immediate problems do not unfavorably constrain future options.

▷Strategy processes can serve an important role as a change agent in the organization. By providing a forum within which objectives are examined and information about the external environment is collected and evaluated, the strategy process promotes the revision of existing assumptions and suggests agendas for future consideration. Moreover, a strategy process can focus management's attention on ends rather than means, on effectiveness rather than efficiency, and on what is good for the entire organization and not just its parts.

▷Strategy processes can be important in preparing for contingencies or opportunities, and for protecting or expanding margins of safety that organizations require in their operations. Since the process often is designed to provide early warning of changes in the external environment, it can help the organization create new options for coping with these changes.

▷Strategy processes help organizations resist the natural tendency to become prisoners of their own traditions. In fact, the process itself can become the learning mechanism through which management attention at all levels is focused on the future and through which a philosophy of future-orientedness encompasses the entire organization. The strategy process contributes to organizational learning by extending the time horizons of decision makers, broadening their perspectives, allowing for the sharing of assumptions and values, and facilitating the development and use of future-oriented information flows.

Not just any strategy process will achieve these benefits. Many in use today are too mechanical, too rigid, and too heavily focused on short-term results to be of much value in organizational learning. When this is the case, it is not surprising to find the process in disrepute, inert and irrelevant, ignored by executives. But the solution is not to destroy it, as some organizations have done, but to change its nature. Strategy processes must be flexible, open, future-oriented, and focused on the interface between the organization and its environments.

Such an approach is illustrated by the process currently being used by the Southern California Edison Company (SCE). According to Glenn J. Bjorklund, a vice president, a review of strategic planning efforts at the electric utility from 1965 through 1985 showed them to be seriously flawed. Like most other companies, Edison was too rigidly tied to projections of historical trends. When unexpected events occurred, such as the large increase in oil costs following the Arab oil embargo in 1973 or the passage of the Air Quality Act in 1976, the carefully developed strategies were rendered useless. Indeed, none of the plans developed over this period turned out as they were envisioned at the time of preparation.

SCE's current strategy process is called "Strategies for an Uncertain Future." The first step was the preparation of twelve different scenarios for the period from 1987 to 1997. For example, one of the scenarios, labeled "High Fuel Cost," assumes a reemergence of OPEC control over oil pricing, disruption of oil supply lines resulting from conflicts in the Middle East, and greater government regulation, including restrictions on coal use due to acid rain. Another scenario envisions an economic boom in the company's service area, while a third is based on expanded environmental restrictions.

Preparation of the twelve scenarios is an example of an activity that, although still rare, is becoming more necessary for American corporations. Sometimes referred to as futures research, environmental scanning, or issues analysis, its purpose is to develop an understanding of the fundamental causes and directions of possible changes in an organization's future environments.

With such an understanding the organization can focus on when and where decisions are necessary so as to prepare for change over a five- to twenty-year (or more) time horizon. Forecasting is an integral part of this activity, but not its prime objective. While forecasting is limited to determining what is *likely* to happen, futures research is much broader, encompassing what *can* happen and what various stakeholders think *should* happen. Indeed, much of futures research is devoted to determining what can be done to prevent certain forecasts from coming true or to facilitate realization of desirable forecasts.

Through futures research a leader can learn what is worth forecasting—that is, those trends or occurrences that would truly make a difference in selecting a strategy. Similarly, he can explore how sensitive contemplated action alternatives may be to the accuracy of the forecasts. Futures research also helps identify issues that should be brought to the organization's attention for policy purposes; assesses the impact of trends on key organizational areas; and articulates images of desirable futures out of which visions, objectives, and goals can be fashioned.

SCE's next step was to analyze the implications of each scenario for what resources the company would need. One of the twelve scenarios was taken as a base case, a sort of business-as-usual situation in which electricity demand grew at 2 percent per year. By analyzing each scenario's fuel costs, economic growth assumptions, environmental constraints, and so forth, it was found that resource requirements could vary as much as 5,000 megawatts in either direction from the base case, depending on which scenario actually occurred.

Out of this analysis came a new vision for the company that stressed flexibility of response. The aim was to make it easy to adapt to a wide range of possible changes in the firm's environment. SCE created a flexible portfolio of electricity sources. In addition to their existing generating facilities, they arranged for variable power purchases from other utilities, cogeneration with corporate clients, hydroelectricity, biomass, solar, geothermal, and wind farms. In doing so, they reduced their dependence on oil, gas, and coal as fuels and increased their ability to store energy generated at off-peak periods. Edison now has what I called in the previous chapter a robust strategy that will sustain it through great variations and unexpected changes in its operating environment.

This type of strategy process can be a powerful instrument for anticipatory learning if it concentrates on longer-term issues and brings leaders and followers together to share their beliefs and contemplate new directions. The organization learns much about what it is, where it is going, and what it might have to deal with along the way. An organization may be able to get along on its own for a while without such a process, but only at great risk.

INITIATIVE: SPARKING
ORGANIZATIONAL INNOVATION

An organization that leads is the pacesetter among its

peers. It is often the most innovative in its group. If not the technological leader, it may be the most innovative in providing customer service, adding value to its products and services, or reaching new standards of quality and performance. The leading organization is the one that makes *new* things happen, that pushes its peers or its industry to new heights.

In recent years, Japanese companies have become leaders in such industries as banking, consumer electronics, and automobiles. How these firms rose to leadership is no mystery, for among the things they made happen were:

- constant improvements in products and services, often obsoleting their own before competitors did
- full use of technological potential in all operations and products, especially through the use of robots, electronics, and advanced materials
- frequent improvements in management processes, with broad participation in the search for new approaches
- short-term sacrifice and considerable patience for the achievement of market penetration and other long-term goals
- obsession with high quality and customer satisfaction
- hard work, with employees taking as much pride in organizational success as in personal gain
- top-to-bottom commitment to progress, change, and risk taking, including substantial budgets for innovation
- active collection of intelligence on successful innovations by others anywhere in the world, coupled with an eagerness to apply these ideas to their own products and processes

These are hardly great secrets. Peter Drucker, Tom Peters, and dozens of other management scholars and consultants have described how organizations can become more innovative. And those that lead invariably are.

MASTERY OF INTERDEPENDENCE: THE GLOBAL IMPERATIVE

Organizations that lead their peers are expert in fostering interdependence internally and externally. Internally, these organizations benefit from collective judgments that embody the best thinking available to the group. If a group is characterized by mutual trust, teamwork, and openness to change, it is more likely to be able to manage complexity in its environment. It will be easier for it to develop appropriate assumptions about the future; easier to reach agreement on actions; and easier to coordinate responses to change. Most important, the need for control diminishes with true interdependence as people become better able to self-organize to meet new challenges.

Consider IBM's dominance in the computer industry, which is due in no small part to human resources policies designed to create interdependence and loyalty. IBM hires good people, spends vast sums to develop them, and promotes almost entirely from within. The IBM culture, including its famous dress code and reluctance to lay people off, is designed to create a feeling of "family." This feeling is reinforced by a paternalistic, exceptionally generous benefits program. For example, IBMers can get up to five weeks of vacation; assistance with mortgage financing or child adoption; up to $5,000 for training for new careers after retirement; and a college scholarship program that can finance up to $32,000 of their children's education. As a result, IBM's turnover rate is among the lowest in the country, and its employee morale is among the highest. The firm has an enviable record of teamwork, loyalty, and innovation.

Interdependence also extends to other stakeholders. The closer an organization can get to its customer or client community, the better it can serve that community, the easier it is to outflank competitors, and the more likely it will be to receive early warning of changes in needs and attitudes. American unions have at long last come to realize how dependent their own success is on the success of their employers, and vice versa. Japanese firms have demonstrated conclusively that great benefits are to be gained by establishing stable long-term relationships with a small core of suppliers, thereby building a mutual stake in the success of the final product. Similarly, considerable benefits can be realized from close ties with financial institutions, local communities, universities and high schools, and trade associations.

But it is at the international level where interdependence is becoming the key to organizational leadership. With near-instantaneous communications, efficient transportation, aggressive international banks, and converging consumer tastes, all forces point toward the global integration of organizations. Those who would lead their peers will have to draw resources—financial, human, and technical—from all over the globe; operate successfully in many nations; and relate comfortably to a variety of constituencies, including international, national, and local governmental bodies, a multicultural work force, and multilingual customer and supplier communities. Those who aspire to leadership in the next decade have already taken giant steps in this direction. For example:

▷The Ford Motor Company, recently the most profitable car company in the world, has been moving deliberately toward a globally integrated company organized around "centers of excellence." The idea is to place project responsibility for a particular automobile or component in the Ford facility with the greatest expertise, wherever in the world it may be located. The work would be done just once for the entire global market. Thus the Ford facility in Brentwood, England, might design compact cars and all four-cylinder engines for Ford worldwide; Detroit would concentrate on larger cars, engines, and automatic transmissions; and the smallest cars would be engineered in Japan. Almost all top executives at Ford already have had significant international experience, and much of the design and manufacturing is team-oriented with considerable global interaction.

▷Olivetti, Europe's leading manufacturer of personal computers, is being remade into a global computer services company that will sell the same products and services worldwide. Global production and marketing is the only way the company can recover large investments in products and services that are needed to compete but that are rapidly being made obsolete by technological progress. Unless it competes head-on with powerful adversaries all over the world, Olivetti will not be able to keep even its local market, because the competitors will grow stronger on the basis of their own global successes.

▷Andreas Stihl, a German company, manufactures chain saws. By concentrating on a narrow niche at the high-cost, high-quality end of the market and carefully cultivating its dealer service network, it has been able to sell 87 percent of its products around the world. In effect, it has become a global leader in its market niche.

Many more examples could be given, but the lesson is clear. Leading organizations must cultivate global interdependence if they wish to survive, let alone lead, in the twenty-first century. This applies not only to high technology but to all products and services. World-class museums now mount exhibits that travel around the world. Television programs and motion pictures are available universally. Advertising, banking, insurance, and many other services are already multinational in scope. In short, the world is rapidly becoming a single, interdependent economy in which only those large organizations able to compete everywhere at once will be able to compete at all.

ORGANIZATIONAL INTEGRITY

Just as individuals must take the high road to earn the right to lead, so must organizations. Customers and other constituencies depend on organizations to perform in a predictable, reliable fashion. They must provide value and deliver quality, acting honorably at every level to inspire confidence in those who would use them as role models. They must adhere to the physician's admonition, "First, and above all, do no harm." Here are a few examples:

▷The J. M. Smucker Company of Orrville, Ohio, dominates the nation's market for jams and jellies with nearly three times the market share of its closest competitor. A family company now run by the fourth generation of Smuckers, it zealously protects its reputation for quality, integrity, and dependability. It fills every jar with a little bit more than the customer pays for. It refuses to advertise on television shows that contain violence, sex, or games of chance. The first in its industry to put nutritional information on every label, Smuckers uses no preservatives or artificial sweeteners despite the fact that competitors attain a cost advantage by doing so. It pays for full-time federal inspectors at every plant—although not required to do so. Ever since the first Mr. Smucker actually signed every label to show he stood behind each product, the company has built a reputation for integrity that has allowed it to be by far the industry leader, despite much larger and better-financed competitors.

▷Johnson & Johnson is consistently ranked an outstanding company. The firm attributes a good part of its success to its "Credo," a statement about its responsibilities to its customers, employees, stockholders, and the local communities where it manufactures its products. Its severest test came in 1982 when seven people died in the Chicago area from

Tylenol capsules laced with cyanide. Although not at fault, Johnson & Johnson immediately recalled all Tylenol capsules throughout the United States as a precaution, replacing them with capsules in newly designed tamper-resistant containers. Although costing over $100 million, this gesture obviously demonstrated high integrity and was widely applauded in the media. It was so effective that within three months the company was able to recapture almost all of its 35 percent market share and to reinforce its image as a company that really cares about people.

▷In stark contrast to Smuckers and Johnson & Johnson is the Manville Corporation. At its peak in the late 1970s, it had revenues of nearly $3 billion from asbestos products and other businesses. However, the first asbestos health lawsuits were filed in 1929, and much evidence has accumulated since then that asbestos could cause death from cancer. Rather than acting in the public interest, Manville took few health precautions, resisted the lawsuits, and suppressed unfavorable information. For example, it failed to label its products with warnings to workers, conducted little research on the health effects of asbestos, and, until the early 1970s, refused to even discuss chest problems with employees. As the result of an obvious lack of integrity in the way they handled the asbestos situation, Manville became the target of consumerist and environmentalist groups, was sued by hundreds and then thousands of past workers, and finally in 1982 filed for bankruptcy.

Unlike Manville, organizations that lead their peers typically are respected for high standards of integrity as much as for any other aspect of their performance. In such organizations, all constituencies are treated fairly in exchange for their loyalty and trust. The Golden Rule applies to all interactions, and an ethic of caring and sharing is part of the culture. This will become even more necessary in the complex, fast-moving world of the future, where quick decisions will have to be based on trust and integrity. If a matter ends up in a lawsuit, the organization has already lost a great deal, even if it wins the suit.

BALANCED GROWTH

No organization is guaranteed a leadership position. Yet in the new age of leadership, an organization will have to sustain a position at the forefront of its peer group, or at least be a major contender for leadership, if it is not to face inevitable decline. This follows from the fact that only the organizations that lead will have the stature, philosophy, and resources to attract the most talented and dedicated employees and to build the human and organizational capital necessary to deal with confounding complexity and rapid change.

Leading organizations will be future-oriented; operate at an appropriate scale; learn through the strategy process; develop a distinctive competence; be innovative; stress quality and value added; exploit interdependence creatively; and develop a high sense of organizational integrity. Those who say this costs too much do not realize that these are not costs at all; rather, they are essential investments in the future without which an organization will have no future.

These arguments presuppose an America that is itself a successful world leader and supportive of organizational leadership. If the country is staggering under high debt and interest rates; if it cannot educate its young people well, protect its environment or renew its infrastructures; if it is selling off its assets at fire-sale rates and encouraging hollow corporations; then organizational leadership is much more difficult.

But is it possible for the United States to exercise a leadership role in an interdependent world, and if so, how? That is the subject to which we now turn our attention.

10

AMERICAN LEADERSHIP IN THE TWENTY-FIRST CENTURY

"Build today, then, strong and sure,
With a firm and ample base;
And ascending and secure
Shall tomorrow find its place."

—Henry Wadsworth Longfellow, "The Builders"

BACK IN THE 1930s, Will Rogers could always get a laugh by reminding his audience, "Last year we said things can't go on like this, and they didn't. They got worse."

Today the national dialogue is full of concern about declining competitiveness, mounting debt burdens, and loss of national will. Will the United States retreat or regenerate? Will we expire or explode in a new surge of growth and dynamism? Will we lead or lag behind those nations rushing to stake out positions in the global information society of the twenty-first century?

The answers are not at all obvious. America has great

assets but also great liabilities in seeking a renaissance of leadership. Consider the following:

- We have a highly productive economy, but our productivity is not growing fast enough to be competitive in key manufacturing industries.
- We have abundant natural resources, but we suffer from an overabundance of environmental problems.
- With the highest gross national product in the world, we still have rampant poverty, crime, and homelessness in our urban slums.
- Our colleges and universities are among the best in the world, but our high school dropout rates, illiteracy, and test scores have created what many call a crisis in education.
- We spend billions to successfully build up and protect Europe and Japan from military threats but then have to turn around and borrow billions from them to maintain our standard of living, mostly by importing products that could and should have been produced here in the first place.
- We are first-rate in making scientific discoveries but increasingly second-rate in realizing their economic potential.
- We have a vibrant entrepreneurial sector that is the envy of the world in creating new jobs, but many of our major corporations seem more interested in eliminating jobs than investing in new ones.

It is as if America has reached a sort of midlife crisis. We look at ourselves and argue that we're not slipping but some of the younger upstarts—whom, after all, we financed, trained, nurtured, and protected—have caught up to us and are beginning to move ahead. We know we're still pretty strong, and we think we have what it takes to reassert our leadership at any time, but it's not as easy as it once was. Besides, we're pretty comfortable, and maybe we should begin thinking about mellowing out. Or maybe we should be doing something else. On the other hand, . . .

The classic response to a midlife crisis is a new challenge or, in the words of *The Godfather,* an offer that can't be refused. American leadership is truly needed in the world, perhaps now more than ever. The alternative to leadership is not a mellow status quo but a persistent erosion in the standard of living, increasing dependency on foreign creditors, and a growing despair about ever being able to improve our quality of life.

But why have leadership at all? History has shown that civilization makes substantial progress only when some form of leadership unifies nations, helps resolve disputes, and stabilizes the international order. At various times, that leadership came from Athens, Rome, the Vatican, Spain, Great Britain, or elsewhere. Of course, it was often imposed by military force, an option no longer available and certainly not desirable.

In the absence of leadership, the next several decades may well be marked by excessive global instability as each nation seeks to protect its own interests at the expense of its competitors. With destructive competition, no voice for cohesion, or even a common set of rules, there would be frequent realignments of military and economic power blocks, excessive power in the hands of multinational corporations, and heightened unpredictability, making it very difficult for all organizations and institutions to plan or even to function.

International leadership in the twenty-first century is likely to be different from the historical model. Military strength will count less, economic strength far more. All nations will be much more integrated and interdependent on a shrinking planet, with actions taken at any one place having effects everywhere at once. The Asian giants will discover their international clout—especially China, Japan, and India—and major decisions will require a larger set of more equal multilateral powers. It will be much less possible for one nation to "win" if doing so means that another "loses."

Under these conditions, successful international leadership will depend on coordination, coalition-building, persuasion, and compromise to find directions that enhance the well-being of all nations. It definitely will not succeed with authoritarianism, coercion, imperialism, or manipulation of some nations for the benefit of others.

America does have what it takes for this kind of leadership—a strong domestic market to which all other nations desire access, and a vibrant free-enterprise system. It has plentiful natural resources, making it less dependent on foreign sources of raw materials than other economically strong nations are. The work force is diverse and innovative, and the social culture is open to change and respects hard work and success. The political structure is stable and supports important, widely admired values such as freedom, equal opportunity, and respect for human dignity. And America does have a track record of generally benign leadership, having helped rebuild the broken nations of Japan and in Europe, provided generous assistance to underdeveloped nations, successfully prevented nuclear exchanges for forty years, and led the world into the information age.

Besides, as we look around, we see no other viable candidate for world leadership. America is the only nation that is among the big three both economically (along with Japan and the EEC) and militarily (along with the USSR and China). It is a superpower with a leadership track record, while every other strong nation has serious handicaps to overcome in asserting leadership. Moreover, there is no international body that can assume a leadership role, including the United Nations, which works only when the superpowers agree and no vital interests of strong nations are affected.

So it appears that American leadership will be an important factor in the next several decades. But to be a leader, some changes will have to be made to accommodate the new realities we have been discussing. To maintain its international leadership, and to use it wisely and well, America must be seen by others as having its own house in order, both now and into the twenty-first century. This means, among other things, that America must be militarily secure; economically strong; capable of operating at the cutting edge of progress and innovation; in possession of a compelling vision of its own future; and truly concerned with the future of the entire world, not just its own people. The key to achieving that position lies in the seven megaskills. In this chapter, we will discuss farsightedness and mastery of change, leaving the other five megaskills for the next chapter.

FARSIGHTEDNESS: NATIONAL FORESIGHT

Americans always have been of two minds when it comes to national planning as a way of addressing vital long-term issues. One could imagine the Supreme Court being called upon to judge whether planning is properly a part of the American tradition. First, one side argues that there have been incredible feats of vision, planning, and long-range thinking throughout our history. For example, they say, consider the following:

- The American Constitution itself is a powerful and much-admired plan for the long-term evolution of a free society. With its strict guarantees of freedom and delicate balancing of power, it allows for the preservation of tradition while offering great flexibility for change and adaptation.
- The construction of canals, massive flood-control projects, rural electrification, the national park system, the

interstate highway system, and the space program were all examples of successful long-range thinking on a grand scale.

• The social security system, savings bonds, and the Marshall Plan were social inventions that institutionalized short-term sacrifices for long-term national benefits.

"No," say our imaginary Supreme Court justices, "that's not the tradition." Then the other side argues that Americans have a strong *anti*-planning tradition. They have been brought up on Horatio Alger tales of entrepreneurial success and myths of rugged individualism. They have a strong belief in the "invisible hand," convinced that the long-term interest of the nation is best served by millions of people pursuing their own self-interest, guided only by impersonal market forces. They have little confidence in civil servants or politicians, for they fear and distrust big government. They especially don't want Washington to tell them what to do. And all this is reinforced by a genuine revulsion at the kind of centralized planning and control typical of communist countries. So the tradition must be anti-planning, mustn't it?

"No," says the mythical Supreme Court, "that's not the tradition, either." Now both sides are frustrated. "It must be one or the other," they say. "This indecision has led to continued conflict. Nobody knows whether national planning is acceptable or how much the American people will support. Lack of a national vision makes it tough for individuals and organizations to do their own planning. It puts us at a disadvantage relative to Japan and other countries that do have their long-term act together. And because administrations change every four or eight years, other nations are uncertain about what they can depend on us to do. It is tearing us apart and undermining our ability to lead." The sage Supreme Court justices would then reply, "That's it. That's the tradition!"

In actual practice, these conflicting views have led to wide swings in the public's attitude toward national planning and farsightedness. In times of national crisis, depression or war, planning and even extensive regulation are accepted without much fuss. In less trying times, long-range activities still may be acceptable if tied to some clear national purpose such as "the war on poverty" or the space program. Some types of planning are always accepted—for example, military planning for new weapons systems. On the other hand, in the past decade there has been a sweeping reaction to long-range activities in many government departments (e.g., housing, environment, agriculture) and massive disengagement in others, as typified by deregulation in the transportation and energy fields. America remains the least committed of all industrialized nations to long-range thinking.

Thus it appears that Americans don't want a totally *unplanned society*, for they understand the value of long-range thinking in some areas. They definitely don't want a *planned society*, especially if that means more government control over their activities. However, they are willing to accept a *society that plans*, as long as the scope of the planning is confined to areas that can't be handled adequately in the private sector and are vital to the nation's long-term health and survival.

We are now at a watershed point where a great increase in farsightedness is needed if America is to continue to exercise a global leadership role. There is an accumulation of unmet long-term needs both in the United States and the world including, for example, environmental issues, decaying or nonexistent infrastructures, population growth, poverty, and homelessness. With the recent lessening of tensions between the superpowers, this is an ideal time to begin addressing these long-term issues.

Even more important, however, is the need for positive visions of the future—a new American dream to inspire a new generation of young people to public service and leadership. No nation can lead unless it knows where it is going. Indications that the nation has lost its sense of direction include low voter turnouts, the erosion of American competitiveness, and decrease in optimism about the future (discussed in the first chapter).

The U.S. government can do much to help individuals and organizations, both domestic and international, plan for their own futures. Following is a list of some specific actions that would greatly improve national foresight and still be fully consistent with American traditions.

1. Create and support national "outlook institutions." The U.S. Office of Technology Assessment (OTA), established in 1972 in the legislative branch, is a prototype for the kind of public agency that could greatly increase farsightedness. OTA conducts and sponsors impartial studies on the long-term implications of technological choices facing the nation. For example, it has issued influential reports on the technologies of energy, agriculture, materials, health, computers, and transportation. In its studies, OTA collects and evaluates long-term technological forecasts, examines the feasibility and anticipated social impacts of potential technological policy options that should be considered, and communicates the results to legislators and the general public. It is purely an advisory body, with no power to implement its ideas.

OTA, which is only modestly supported at the present time, deserves greater funding. Other "outlook institutions" are needed in both the executive and legislative branches to provide similar services in such areas as economic policy, education, defense, health care, and communications.

2. Develop better mechanisms for national pathfinding and direction-setting. New democratic processes are needed for helping national leaders search for new directions. To some extent, this has been happening at the state and local levels as part of "Year 2000" conferences and projects to stimulate citizen participation with experts in dialogues about the future. However, these discussions have no counterparts at the national or international level.

Instead, ideologically oriented think tanks have grown influential in framing public issues along partisan grounds. National political campaigns, which should provide alternative visions of the future from which the electorate could choose, instead often degenerate into personality contests, mudslinging, and desperate attempts to align themselves with immediate concerns as expressed in the latest public opinion polls. A well-educated and concerned citizenry deserves better.

3. Sponsor long-range global studies. In 1977, President Carter ordered a comprehensive, multidepartmental study of "the probable changes in the world's population, natural resources and environment through the end of the century." The final report, called *The Global 2000 Report to the President*, appeared in 1980. Although it was totally ignored by the Reagan administration, it has had considerable impact elsewhere in the world. Similar studies were commissioned in some other nations, and a global controversy about the prospects for the planet was sparked that continues to this day. Whatever the technical merits of its conclusions, *The Global 2000 Report* demonstrated the need for this kind of information and the opportunity it provides to the United States for exercising a leadership role in the consideration of world issues.

America is uniquely positioned by virtue of its expertise, data bases, and institutional resources to conduct these kinds of global studies. By doing so, it can provide the knowledge, information, and policy analyses necessary for joint international initiatives to improve the world's condition, not just environmentally but in health, trade, agriculture, and in a variety of other areas as well. As an important side benefit, such studies stimulate the development of techniques and skills in long-range forecasting and planning and promote the exploration of long-range issues throughout the nation's educational system at every level.

4. Organize for long-range thinking at every level of government. In 1974, the U.S. House of Representatives passed the so-called foresight provision, which provided that each committee of the House "shall on a continuing basis undertake futures research and forecasting on matters within the jurisdiction of that committee." Though the move was a step in the right direction, and the Congressional Research Service of the Library of Congress set up a Futures Research Group to help, the provision has not yet had a major impact. The executive branch, especially under President Reagan, had little interest in long-range thinking and was dead opposed to anything resembling national planning.

For farsightedness to become a part of American leadership, it will have to permeate all government agencies and institutions, especially those concerned primarily with policy rather than administration. There are many ways this could happen, including new positions in the Executive Office of the President concerned with long-range policy matters; the assignment of responsibilities for foresight to the Council of Economic Advisors, the Office of Management and Budget, and other agencies; the preparation of an annual Future State of the Union Address; the establishment of a quasi-governmental entity similar to the Swedish Secretariat for Futures Studies; or the establishment of centers of excellence in long-range policy research at major universities.

More than any specific proposal, farsightedness is an attitude. It is a frame of mind that declares that America is deeply concerned and feels personal responsibility for the world's future; is willing to lead in the search for new opportunities to improve international conditions; is committed to constantly monitoring and assessing global changes so as to receive early warning of issues that may require attention; and is resolved to act proactively rather than reactively in response to critical emerging issues. It is an attitude that has yet to take hold in the American political system but one that is consistent with the best traditions of this nation, and a cornerstone of any attempt to retain global leadership.

MASTERY OF CHANGE: ECONOMIC RENEWAL

I started this chapter by saying that in order for a nation to be a leader, it must be militarily secure and economically strong among other nations. As the Cold War thaws the United States has a golden opportunity to divert resources from military to economic concerns without compromising its own security. This process of economic renewal and industrial renaissance, if successfully guided, could provide a model for other nations and would be a fine example of U.S. leadership.

It has become obvious in recent years that the nature of the military threat to the United States is changing. The USSR, while still an adversary that bears close watching, is becoming markedly less dangerous to the United States. It has a new leadership apparently more committed to internal development than to external aggression. It has a nuclear deterrent so powerful and secure that it is able to negotiate mutual arms reduction agreements without threatening its own security. Costly failures in Afghanistan and elsewhere have tempered its appetite for military adventurism, especially when its own anemic economy is competing with the military for scarce resources. It desperately needs infusions of Western capital and technology. The Soviet Union must realize that a continuation of the arms race could bankrupt it long before it gains any real military advantage, so it has a strong motivation to negotiate force reductions.

Meantime, America faces threats from other directions—arms proliferation, terrorism, the international drug trade. Fortunately, these threats don't require massive investments in SDI, Stealth Bombers, Minuteman and MX missiles, and the other paraphernalia of a nuclear confrontation.

Moreover, the time certainly has come to share the U.S. military burden with allies who benefit from it as much or more than we do and who are well able to afford their fair share of the costs. For example, a major beneficiary of U.S. protection of Persian Gulf oil is Japan, which spends only 1 percent of its GNP on defense, while we spend 6 percent. Americans are becoming less willing to subsidize the Japanese while they use their capital to buy up blue-chip real estate in Honolulu, Los Angeles, and New York. Similarly, we can no longer afford to go into debt in order to spend $150 billion each year to defend a prosperous Europe.

America's massive defense establishment consumes over 80 percent of the discretionary spending of the federal budget—i.e., that part not already committed to interest on the national debt or mandated entitlements and transfer payments. A portion of these funds could surely be better spent in improving competitiveness, strengthening the economy, reducing debt, or providing other vital services. Our motivation to reduce defense expenditures is almost as great as that of the Soviets.

So the first thing America has to do to reassert its global leadership is to manage the transition from investment in defense to investment in the economy and society. The second is to control and reduce our various debt burdens. The total national debt of more than $2 trillion costs about 20 percent of each year's federal budget to service and could cost much more if interest rates go up or the deficits are not tamed. Meanwhile, business and household debt has also exploded, each exceeding $3 trillion, and could prove catastrophic in the event of a severe recession.

The economy is vulnerable because of these debts and will be for many years to come. Historically, debtors aren't leaders; the one who holds the loans calls the shots. With escalating foreign debt, much of America's diplomatic effort of the past few years was devoted to getting other nations to make concessions in our favor—accepting a cheaper dollar, buying more U.S. goods, finding ways to postpone writing off Third World debts, etc. These are signs of weakness, not of leadership. The situation can't get better until the debt situation is clearly being brought under control. Americans will simply have to learn how to save more and produce more and better products if the national house is to be put in order.

The third thing the United States has to do to strengthen its economic growth prospects is to develop coherent and effective industrial policies that enhance U.S. competitiveness in world markets. No longer is the question *whether* there should be national industrial policies, but, rather, *what kind?* For years, the federal government has intervened in the marketplace through regulation, bailouts, favorable tax treatment, antitrust rules, import protection, job training, export loan guarantees, antidumping laws, trade agreements, and other means. Even the Reagan administration, more ideologically committed to free trade than any administration in decades, imposed significant new trade restrictions, or tightened existing tariffs and quotas, on products ranging from sugar, textiles, and lumber to autos, steel, and semiconductors.

The problem is that these interventions have been opportunistic, inconsistent, sometimes counterproductive, and often characterized by lags and lurches that made it difficult for producers to plan and for investors to make commitments. The adversarial relationship between American business and government has begun to hurt. By comparison, our competitors in Japan, Germany, and elsewhere often have benefited from joint business, labor, and government collaboration to enhance the competitiveness of their industries.

An important symptom of this problem lies in industrial

productivity. Though highly productive, the American economy's growth in output per employee has been stagnating, with growth of less than 1 percent per year for the past fifteen years compared to more than twice that in the prior decade. By comparison, productivity in Japan, Great Britain, Norway, Germany, and Sweden has been growing at two to three times the American rate, and the newly industrialized countries have been doing even better. Productivity growth is important because it determines how competitive American products will be in world markets and how much profit will be available for reinvestment or debt reduction. Ultimately, it determines what standard of living will be enjoyed by U.S. workers and consumers.

Perhaps nothing would provide clearer evidence that America was getting its economic house in order than a rational, consistent, and effective national industrial policy. It need not, and should not, be the province of a few bureaucrats in Washington or an elite cadre of economists. Instead, there should be real representation by all sectors of the economy—workers, managements, investors, consumers, and all levels of government. Choices will have to be made and priorities set; most important, there must be clarity in the distinction between means and ends. As Robert Reich said in *The Next American Frontier*:

> The only sensible end of a nation's economic policy should be improving its citizens' standard of living. The concept of "standard of living" is, of course, vague and subjective. But most people would agree that it is comprised of at least three elements: the goods and services bought by the nation's citizens; the availability of goods that are not purchased directly but that weigh heavily in most people's sense of well-being, such as clean air and water, protection from crime and accident, and security against medical or financial disaster; and, finally, the sense that these

goods and services, both public and private, are justly shared among citizens. Such economic goals as growth, higher productivity, lower inflation, and a strong currency are means of achieving a higher standard of living, but they are not ends in themselves.

These three processes—diverting some funds from military to economic expenditures in the federal budget, reducing the nation's vulnerability to debt, and evolving a more effective national industrial policy—would greatly increase America's ability to exercise global leadership. They would certainly defuse the insistence of our trading partners that we get our economic house in order and would give us much more freedom to coordinate and influence international economic policies.

Thus far, I have focused on farsightedness and change. As essential as they are to America's long-term leadership, they are only the beginning. Nothing less than a major restructuring of important elements of U.S. society will suffice. It is not just the USSR that needs "perestroika." We need our own version—a "perestroika Americana."

11

PERESTROIKA AMERICANA

*"Don't be afraid to take a big step if one is indicated.
You can't cross a chasm in two small jumps."*

—David Lloyd George

A HUNGARIAN FOLKTALE tells of a wise old man walking down a country lane with a group of students. "Look at that tree full of birds," he said as he threw a stone to roust the flock. "Now, look again," he said after the birds had settled in the branches. "That's how the world changes." "But we don't understand," his pupils demanded, "all the birds are back." "Ah," said the old man with a knowing smile, "but each is sitting on a different branch."

Lately it seems as if America sees change in just this way—a little budget increase here, a small tax cut there, but woe to anyone who wants real structural change. In the last several presidential elections, the candidates ran on personality, character, patriotism, image, competency—almost anything they could think of to avoid having to address the structural changes necessary to retain U.S. leadership in the world.

But we can't continue to borrow from the future to sustain outmoded structures. It is time to make some hard choices and commitments, some of which will be suggested in this chapter.

INSTITUTIONAL DESIGN: AMERICA'S DISTINCTIVE COMPETENCE

In the twenty-first century, every nation, no matter how large or powerful, will have to search diligently for its own distinctive competence. This determines the relative strengths of each nation not just in trade and finance but also in terms of international relations and world esteem.

The United States doesn't seem to have reached a national consensus yet on its distinctive competence. What can we excel at in the next few decades? What do we want to do and what can we do better than any other nation on earth? If we were clearer on these matters, we would be in a far better position to design the institutional and social structures and policies that could support them.

Two current candidates for America's distinctive competence seem destined to be less important for the United States in the next several decades. One is military weapons. For years, America has been arsenal to the world, supplying everything from tanks and fighter aircraft to small arms in massive quantities to dozens of client states around the world. This market may be approaching saturation and, in any event, strong foreign competitors, such as France, Israel, England, and the USSR, now exist. Given world developments, it is hard to see how a further expansion of American emphasis on weaponry could enhance our leadership in the next several decades.

The second candidate for distinctive competence that may not grow in importance in the future is agriculture. American farmers are probably the most productive in the

world, so much so that we are plagued by perennial sur-
pluses except in years of severe drought. However, many
nations that are potential customers for these crops are
averse to becoming dependent on foreign suppliers for food,
especially major grain crops. They prefer long-term self-
reliance, even if it imposes large costs on them to subsidize
inefficient farmers. Besides, many of them are short on
foreign exchange and have no alternative employment to
offer their farmers if they were to import more of their food.
Meantime, America is meeting strong competition from
Australia, Argentina, and other food exporters for the
international agricultural markets that do exist. America's
strength in agriculture, while remaining significant, is not
likely to increase our leadership potential in the years
ahead.

Where, then, is our distinctive competence, and what can
we do to build institutions and policies to support it? I
would argue that there are four areas of surpassing importance in the twenty-first century in which America has all
the necessary resources and incentives to lead the world: (1)
information and communication technologies and services;
(2) biotechnology and health care; (3) energy conservation;
and (4) environmental protection. The reasons for these
choices and some of their institutional implications are
discussed in the following sections.

Information/Communication Technologies and Services

The well-documented Information Society rapidly
spreading across the globe is the leading edge of economic
development into the next century. It is a major factor in the
expansion of global awareness and interdependence. This
technology is rapidly expanding human intelligence; restructuring the economy of developed nations; creating a
myriad of new products and services; revitalizing the public
sector; redesigning most jobs; and altering expectations
about future possibilities for civilization.

By virtue of its dominance in space communications, computer and telecommunications hardware and software, and information bases, America is peculiarly well positioned to lead this development. The United States is also world-class in entertainment, the graphic arts, publishing, and computer-aided design and engineering. It has more computer power in the hands of its people and more millions of man-years of hands-on programming experience than any other nation. And it has a powerful advantage in the worldwide use of English as the international language of both business and computer science.

However, much remains for us to do to protect our position in this area. We need to regain leadership of the computer chip industry and reenter the consumer electronics field, now virtually abandoned to Japan, in order to provide the industrial base for developing low-cost, high-quality electronics manufacturing. A national Department (or Institute) of Information and Communications should be established to develop and disseminate detailed statistics on these industries, to develop forecasts and recommend government initiatives in this area, to stimulate and fund long-range research and development, and to provide export assistance.

We should also develop a national information policy to manage the evolution of the Information Society in the public interest. For example, such a policy would protect the rights and property of all users and suppliers of information and guarantee that information about individuals is not used in any way to violate their privacy or dignity. It would provide for fuller use of information technology in delivering social services. It would assure that information resources are not concentrated in the hands of a small powerful elite but made available to all citizens and nonprofit organizations regardless of economic or educational disadvantage. Only then would it be possible to stimulate the information industries while avoiding a societal split into the information-rich and the information-poor.

Biotechnology and Health Care

American scientists have made many of the major breakthroughs in biotechnology that will serve as the basis for
multibillion-dollar world markets in pharmaceuticals,
medical diagnostics, agriculture, materials, nutrition, and
other fields for years to come. We have the necessary breadth
and depth, with well-established technical resources and
multinational corporations able to exploit discoveries
quickly worldwide. With an expanding population of senior citizens, the most health-conscious people in the
world, and health care bills that are already a substantial
and growing part of the GNP, there is every incentive to
place high priority in these areas. And, certainly, any
nation that makes a substantial contribution toward improving health care and reducing disease, early death, and
suffering worldwide would be a strong candidate for global
leadership.

Of course, other nations have recognized this potential as
well. Some have given this area high priority in access to
resources and have facilitated its development and commer-
cialization, often using American technology to do so. As
Earle Harbison, Jr., president of Monsanto, told a Senate
committee recently, biotechnology in the United States "is
still perceived primarily as a regulatory and legal problem,
not an economic opportunity. . . . Much effort is being
expended to see that nothing goes wrong, but little effort is
being expended to see that things go right." Harbison is not
kidding; among the agencies influencing the development
or use of biotechnology are the EPA, USDA, FDA, OSHA,
and NIH, not to mention state regulatory agencies and the
ever-present threat of lawsuits and court action. An estimated seven thousand biotechnology patents are currently
pending, and it can take two years to get an export license
for already-approved products.

Structural changes are needed to coordinate and simplify
the regulatory process in biotechnology and health care and

to stimulate and strengthen the U.S. lead in this area. There should be an increased emphasis on prevention and testing in health care. Increased research and development funding in biogenetics is needed, including new production processes and expanded monitoring of worldwide developments in this field. Finally, there should be a network of regional corporate, university, and government consortia or centers of excellence to facilitate the discovery and rapid deployment of new applications of these. technologies. These centers would work with doctors and hospitals the way the land grant agricultural colleges work with farmers.

Energy Conservation

There are many reasons why America should seek leadership in energy conservation. We are a major oil consumer, but U.S. oil production is falling more than 3 percent per year while demand rises at 1.8 percent, making us increasingly dependent on foreign suppliers. Imported oil cost us $42 billion in 1987 and could easily exceed $75 billion annually in a few years.

Reducing our oil dependency would not only go far toward improving the trade balance but would make it less necessary to have a military presence in the Middle East and would have beneficial effects on air quality, the greenhouse effect, and employment, all of which will help our international position. Besides, it is difficult to be an economic world leader when we have a reputation for the profligate waste of the world's nonrenewable fossil fuels.

Becoming oil independent is certainly doable. From 1973 to 1986, the U.S. economy grew 33 percent, but energy consumption was virtually flat due to increases in energy efficiency and conservation. Better window insulation *alone* could save the nation more oil and gas than we get from Alaska, according to some estimates. Raising average auto mileage to 42 mpg *alone* would eliminate all current need for imported oil. General Motors is already selling a car (the

Geo Metro) that averages 53 mpg in the city, and Toyota has a five-passenger 98 mpg prototype.

Some $200 billion annually, more than the total trade imbalance, could be saved just by making the United States as energy efficient as Europe or Japan. One or more of the recyclable sources of energy—solar cells, wind generation, biomass, geothermal, or alcohol, for example—could soon become cost competitive with other means of electricity generation, assuming additional research and investments in facilities at an appropriate scale. Many other options exist for a substantial reduction in oil use, including the use of superconductors in electrical transmission, industrial cogeneration, recycling, housing insulation, improved batteries for energy storage, heat pumps, office buildings with windows that open, etc. If all of them were employed to the extent they are economically feasible, there would be little problem in achieving energy independence in less than a decade.

Becoming energy efficient would require several structural changes. The regulatory bias toward large stationary generating sources should be eliminated. A slowly rising tax on all nonrenewable energy resources would raise revenues for investing in alternatives while shifting the economic balance in favor of energy efficiency and alternative fuels. (Any short-term negative effects on low-income people could easily be offset by tax credits or rebates.) Annual subsidies to the nuclear power industry, estimated at $15 billion, should also be reduced. Some of these monies could be invested with large payoffs in research on conservation, renewable fuels, and superconductivity; information dissemination and education; and support to state and local agencies to enhance energy efficiencies in their own operations. Regulatory policy should concentrate on energy efficiency by setting minimum levels of performance for cars, air conditioners, furnaces, and home insulation and internalizing any environmental costs of energy used.

If these actions were taken, the nation's massive foreign oil bill would dwindle, and tens of thousands of new jobs would be created in the United States. As we become skilled in these areas, enormous opportunities for exporting products and services would open up. Examples would include energy-efficient appliances, furnaces, generating plants, and recycling facilities; energy instrumentation, controls and software; solar cells; and superconducting materials and transmission equipment.

Environmental Protection

The deterioration of the global environment is destined to become a central concern throughout the world for many years to come. All of the issues listed in Figure 3 (p. 36)—deforestation, water, species preservation, climate, the ozone layer, etc.—as well as toxic waste disposal, nuclear accidents, and other threats to the global ecology, are matters of concern to all nations inhabiting this small planet.

Because we are a prime contributor to many of the problems and are suffering from them on a grand scale ourselves, America is almost obligated to be a leader in this area. For example, the bill just for cleaning up the radioactive waste from the U.S. weapons program will exceed $100 billion, if it can be done at all. Another example: Most of the northeastern United States is running out of landfills for urban trash, and some cities (like Philadelphia) are already shipping their refuse as far away as Africa. Yet, only America has the technical and financial resources to invest in these areas. Substantial global markets are also available in environmental testing and monitoring devices, pollution control, waste disposal, and habitat preservation, representing tens of thousands of potential new jobs for American workers.

Among the structural changes needed for America to excel in environmental protection are a great expansion of monitoring and information gathering on environmental problems; much closer coordination of federal/state/local environmental initiatives; forcing polluters to pay for adverse environmental effects of their products or production processes; encouraging recycling; combining soil conservation programs with farm supports; investing much more in environmental research; and increasing testing and control of toxic chemicals. At the international level, great opportunity awaits the United States to seek agreements on recycling, population control, reforestation, air and water pollution, and other areas where there is a clear joint interest.

These four areas—information/communication technologies and services, biotechnology and health care, energy conservation, and environmental protection—are prime candidates for America's distinctive competence in the twenty-first century. They are extremely important all over the world now and are destined to become even more so in the years to come. They are areas in which America already has a strong lead, some natural advantages, and, potentially at least, a highly supportive citizenry. Millions of high-tech and low-tech jobs could result. They could certainly become a critical part of America's global leadership in the twenty-first century if given sufficient priority and resources today.

ANTICIPATORY LEARNING: EDUCATIONAL REVITALIZATION

Nothing so fits a nation for leadership in a rapidly changing, information-based future as its educational system. Education is inherently anticipatory, as it is responsible for preparing the next generation for citizenship, employment, and leadership.

Part of the great genius of America is that education has always been recognized as critical by its leaders without regard to political persuasion, as shown in the following quotations:

The preservation of the means of knowledge among the lower ranks is of more importance to the public than all the property of all the rich men in the country.—John Adams

Upon the subject of education . . . I can only say that I view it as the most important subject which we as a people can be engaged in.—Abraham Lincoln

The true prosperity and greatness of a nation is to be found in the elevation and education of its laborers.—Ulysses S. Grant

I see no hope for the world except through education, but I am most optimistic for the world because I believe in education.—Dwight D. Eisenhower

Education . . . is the mainspring of our economic and social progress . . . the highest expression of achievement in our society.—John F. Kennedy

One wonders what these presidents would say if they saw how poorly our education system is performing today (see Figure 10). U.S. performance in math and science is especially dreadful compared to that of the nations with which we must compete technologically in the next two decades. By 1982, the International Association for the Evaluation of Educational Achievement found that seventeen-year-old Americans were in the lowest fourth among their contemporaries in all nations on five of six basic skills in mathematics. In fact, the top 5 percent of American math students did worse than the average Japanese student. In a more recent study reported by the secretary of education, fourteen-year-old Americans placed fourteenth out of seventeen countries in science, tied with Singapore and Thailand. Only 7.5 percent of American high school graduates have enough preparation to take any kind of college science course.

The reasons are not hard to fathom. Fewer than one-

FIGURE 10: SELECTED STATISTICS ON AMERICAN EDUCATION

1. In 1987, according to the Department of Defense, 40 percent of the high school graduates entering the military read at the ninth grade level or below, despite the fact that the military has become much more selective, with some 92 percent of new recruits having at least a high school diploma.

2. In a survey of twenty-one- to twenty-five-year-olds, the National Assessment of Educational Progress (NAEP) found that fewer than 40 percent were able to interpret an article by a newspaper columnist.

3. In a 1986 NAEP study of knowledge of history by seventeen-year-olds, 43 percent could not place World War I between 1900 and 1950, and more than 75 percent did not know within twenty years when Abraham Lincoln was president.

4. In the same study, about one-third of the students could not find the Mississippi River on a map of the United States or France on a map of Europe.

5. In a 1984 study of seventeen-year-olds, NAEP found that fewer than one-fourth could be called adequate on writing tasks considered essential in academic study and business.

6. The nation's average high school dropout rate is over 25 percent, reaching 50 percent in many urban schools, according to the American Association of State Colleges and Universities.

7. Some twenty-three million adults are functionally illiterate, and another forty-seven million are borderline illiterate, according to the National Alliance of Business, which also points out that employers spent over $200 billion in 1987 alone on formal and informal training.

---

third of our high schools even offer a physics course, and more than one-half of our high school graduates have not had even one year of science. Many of our math and science teachers are unqualified, or only marginally qualified, to teach their subjects. Japan, by comparison, attracts some of its most qualified young people into teaching with salaries that are actually higher than those offered to public employees and corporate professionals with similar education. Moreover, while it is not unusual for high school students in most other developed countries to spend eight hours a day at school some 220 days a year, most American schools have a six-hour day for 175 to 180 days per year.

The results are predictable. While the fraction of scientists and engineers in our labor force has declined for two decades, the ratio has doubled in Japan and Germany. The Soviet Union alone now graduates five times as many engineers as the United States.

American universities are actually awarding fewer doctorates in engineering than a decade ago, and half of those awarded are going to foreigners. Though the top 5 percent of America's scientific talent is world-class, our technical depth and breadth is rapidly eroding. In fact, much of the lower 50 percent of our labor pool is functionally illiterate or just barely literate, and some experts estimate that American corporations may already be spending as much as $25 billion annually on remedial education, a cost factored into the price of U.S. products that puts them at a clear competitive disadvantage. It is not surprising that U.S. multinational corporations are increasing the proportion of their research that they do overseas, and that production workers in Japan and Germany are more technically skilled than those in America.

Looking ahead, we find even more problems. Population growth is leveling off and fewer new people are entering the labor force, so job markets are expected to tighten up in the next two decades. More than half of the new jobs in the next decade will require education beyond a high school diploma; yet the new entrants to the labor force will contain a large portion of people who have had the least academic success. Some 35 percent of children now live in poverty; nearly two-thirds come home from school to an empty house; and an ever-increasing proportion are being brought up in families and neighborhoods plagued by alcohol, drugs, delinquency, and low aspirations.

There will be further problems in the teaching pool. The most experienced and highly educated teachers are approaching retirement age or leaving the profession due to burnout or more attractive jobs in industry. In fact, half the nation's teachers leave within seven years of entering the profession to seek higher earnings, greater job satisfaction, and less stress. Those replacing them are often among the least academically qualified college graduates, since other professions offer better pay, working conditions, and growth opportunities to the brighter college students. Misguided academic reforms are adding to the administrative load of teachers, reducing their classroom discretion and job satisfaction.

Unfortunately, the situation can't get much better in the short run. Even heroic measures won't substantially improve the schools, the teaching pool, or the students in the next decade. Virtually all the scientists, engineers, and technicians who will enter the work force in the year 2000 are already in the junior high schools or close to it. For a nation whose competitive advantage depends on technical excellence, this is truly awesome to contemplate.

Thus, despite pious pleadings to the contrary, *the single most important obstacle to American leadership in the twenty-first century is our failing education system.* Nothing less than a crash program to improve the system is needed. Moreover, we know exactly what must be done including, for example, much higher teaching salaries; substantial investments in preschool child care to develop good learning habits early; a national campaign to reduce illiteracy and to upgrade basic skills; much greater emphasis on science and technology at every level; and greater learning demands on students, including more time in school.

Nothing less than total commitment at all governmental levels, as well as full participation by parents, students, and

employers, will turn this situation around. These investments will certainly be expensive, but not nearly so expensive as remedial education, welfare, and crime, lost taxes
from unemployment, less interesting and more stressful
work environments, and the decline of American competitiveness and standard of living if these investments are not
made.

INITIATIVE: ENTREPRENEURSHIP
AND INNOVATION

In contrast to the grim realities discussed in the previous
section, initiative is an area in which America is truly
outstanding. We are a pragmatic, change-oriented, can-do,
take-charge people, and we celebrate and reward those who
make things happen. In particular, our entrepreneurial
sector is the envy of the world. In 1987, while large companies were laying off thousands of people, small companies
with fewer than one hundred workers employed about 30
percent of the labor force and created almost 60 percent of
new jobs. As a result, America's job-creation rate far out-
stripped that of Europe and Japan, even in manufacturing.

It is not simply the hope of high incomes that motivates
entrepreneurs. A *USA Today* survey of the five hundred
fastest-growing privately owned firms in 1986 found that
when asked why they went into business for themselves, 89
percent of the owners marked "desire to control my life," 81
percent marked "desire to be my own boss," 66 percent
"wanted to prove I could do it," and 60 percent marked
"desire to create something new." Only then, in fifth place
with a 55 percent response rate, did the owners say they
went into business "to make money and acquire wealth."
Thus entrepreneurs in America tend to be inherently independent and futures-creative, imparting great energy to the
economy.

The vitality and success of the entrepreneurial sector is so
high that even the largest corporations are trying to recon-

figure themselves to take advantage of the entrepreneurial urges of their workers. This so-called intrapreneurship has allowed some companies like 3M and Johnson & Johnson to maintain exceptional growth rates and to be among the most innovative in their industries worldwide.

In another key area of initiative—research and development—America's record also has been good, but some serious danger signs are beginning to flash. For years, America has been the dominant technological power in the world, spewing out a steady stream of new products, boldly creating new markets, and dramatically improving production processes. We have a long scientific tradition and great research universities. We excel at making the breakthrough discoveries that can create whole new fields of endeavor. We still outspend Japan and Western Europe in R&D, though the gap is closing. Our comparative strength in some key technologies is shown in a recent survey by Booz-Allen & Hamilton (see Figure 11).

However, America has begun to lose some of its technological initiative. For example, the U.S. automobile industry has been painfully slow to apply technological improvements. For years, Detroit dragged its feet on fuel efficiency, emission controls, and radial tires. The use of advanced production methods such as robots and just-in-time delivery systems have seriously lagged behind their application by Japanese competitors.

The auto industry is not alone. The banking industry, public representations to the contrary, is still using software and systems of the sixties and seventies. Apart from a few technological innovations like automated teller machines, U.S. banks still are heavily paper-based and labor-intensive. Even in telecommunications, an industry in which the United States has long been a technological leader, only a fraction of what is possible today has been implemented. Widely discussed applications such as video-conferencing, videotex, electronic mail, and voice messaging are just beginning to have an impact.

FIGURE 11: WHO'S ON TOP IN TECHNOLOGY?

Table shows how executives responded to questions about which country—primarily the U.S. or Japan—leads in various fields of technology. For example, when asked which country leads in supercomputers, 90% of the U.S. executives surveyed answered "the United States" while 10% answered "Japan." In some cases the percentages do not add up to 100%; in almost all those instances the respondents named European nations.

... IN SUPERCOMPUTERS

Survey respondents	Percentage answering "Japan"	Percentage answering "U.S."
U.S. executives:	10%	90%
Japanese executives:	8%	92%
Other Asian executives:	7%	93%

... IN SOFTWARE ENGINEERING?

Survey respondents	Percentage answering "Japan"	Percentage answering "U.S."
U.S. executives:	1.5%	97%
Japanese executives:	2%	98%
Other Asian executives:	6%	91%

... IN ARTIFICIAL INTELLIGENCE AND EXPERT SYSTEMS?

Survey respondents	Percentage answering "Japan"	Percentage answering "U.S."
U.S. executives:	6%	94%
Japanese executives:	8%	92%
Other Asian executives:	15%	85%

... IN COMPUTER-AIDED DESIGN AND ENGINEERING?

Survey respondents	Percentage answering "Japan"	Percentage answering "U.S."
U.S. executives:	21%	79%
Japanese executives:	24%	76%
Other Asian executives:	17%	83%

... IN COMPUTER-INTEGRATED MANUFACTURING?

Survey respondents	Percentage answering "Japan"	Percentage answering "U.S."
U.S. executives:	55%	45%
Japanese executives:	28%	72%
Other Asian executives:	56%	44%

Note: The percentages are based on the replies of 118 U.S. executives, 79 Japanese executives and 66 executives from other Pacific economies.

These are not exceptions. In industry after industry, technological opportunities are being lost to more aggressive foreign firms. Few color televisions, robots, and videocassette recorders are still made in the United States, even though these products originated here. The technological

... IN ROBOTICS?

Survey respondents	Percentage answering "Japan"	Percentage answering "U.S."
U.S. executives:	86%	12%
Japanese executives:	90%	10%
Other Asian executives:	88%	9%

... IN MICROELECTRONICS?

Survey respondents	Percentage answering "Japan"	Percentage answering "U.S."
U.S. executives:	48%	50%
Japanese executives:	78%	22%
Other Asian executives:	52%	48%

... IN HIGH-PERFORMANCE MATERIALS?

Survey respondents	Percentage answering "Japan"	Percentage answering "U.S."
U.S. executives:	29%	64%
Japanese executives:	23%	77%
Other Asian executives:	37%	63%

... IN SUPERCONDUCTIVITY?

Survey respondents	Percentage answering "Japan"	Percentage answering "U.S."
U.S. executives:	10%	87%
Japanese executives:	38%	60%
Other Asian executives:	22%	74%

... IN TELECOMMUNICATIONS (VOICE & DATA)?

Survey respondents	Percentage answering "Japan"	Percentage answering "U.S."
U.S. executives:	11%	84%
Japanese executives:	33%	67%
Other Asian executives:	17%	76%

... IN LASER/FIBER OPTICS?

Survey respondents	Percentage answering "Japan"	Percentage answering "U.S."
U.S. executives:	12%	84%
Japanese executives:	64%	36%
Other Asian executives:	15%	78%

Source: The Times/Booz-Allen & Hamilton survey. *Los Angeles Times*, February 21, 1988, Part IV, 6. Copyright, 1988, *Los Angeles Times*. Reprinted by permission.

initiative in industries as diverse as steel, appliances, railroads, machine tools, and consumer electronics has shifted overseas. Even newer technologies, like superconductivity, are being threatened. As a result, high-technology imports have flooded into the United States.

Foreigners have become more adept not just at producing high-technology goods, but also at innovating. This shows up most dramatically in the patent statistics. From 1961 to 1970, U.S. corporations averaged 34.3 thousand patents per year, while foreign corporations averaged 8.4. From 1971 to 1980, the U.S. statistic had not changed much, but the foreign number had more than doubled to an average of 17.6 thousand patents per year. By 1986, patents to U.S. corporations had actually declined to 29.6 thousand, while foreign corporations had almost caught up at 27 thousand.

The great tragedy is that America's technological strength is eroding just at a time when technology is becoming critically important. Many reasons have been offered for the erosion of American technological initiative:

▷Other nations do a better job of concentrating their national R&D commitments on the commercial sector. In the United States, from 1965 to 1980, federal R&D funds were about equally distributed between military and civilian spending. In the current fiscal year, defense spending is two-thirds of the total R&D budget, the rest being distributed among health, space, and other civilian purposes. Thus, little of the federal investment finds its way into commercial products that can enhance U.S. competitiveness, and many of the nation's best technical minds are captured in military matters.

▷America has no equivalent to Japan's Ministry of International Trade and Industry (MITI), which channels national as well as private-sector R&D expenditures into areas of high national priority, such as superconductivity, microelectronics, artificial intelligence, and biotechnology.

▷American corporations, while sometimes spending more on R&D than their overseas counterparts, employ different criteria for choice of projects. The American firms expect a faster payback on their investment, which often guides their funds toward minor modifications to existing products rather than the creation of whole new markets. During difficult times, such as the recent rash of corporate downsizing, R&D is often cut back, and projects with the longest term potential payoffs are cut first. With less job security, American technical people may have more loyalty to their profession than to their current employers.

▷Technical people do not have as high status in U.S. firms as in their foreign counterparts, perhaps because American firms are usually headed by people with financial, legal, or marketing backgrounds. Engineers and scientists are rarely promoted into top management ranks in large firms.

▷American training in science and engineering is suffering. The number of scientists and engineers per 10,000 in the labor force in 1965 was 64.1 in the United States, 24.6 in Japan, and 22.6 in West Germany. Looking at nonmilitary activities only, one economist in 1977 estimated that the United States had already been surpassed—38 per 10,000 in the United States, 40 in West Germany, and 50 in Japan. By now, with American engineering enrollments declining for the past decade, the absolute numbers must be heavily tilted against us. Moreover, those who do get the jobs are less able than their peers in other countries to monitor and apply technological developments from around the world.

▷Antitrust laws inhibit collaboration among firms in R&D; thus some companies, especially smaller ones, find it difficult to gain access to the latest developments.

There are many things America should do to retain and extend its technological initiative, starting with a much greater investment in technical education at every level. There should be a stronger scientific presence close to the president, either an influential and respected White House science adviser or perhaps a cabinet-level Department of Science and Technology. Much more emphasis in the federal R&D budget should be on technologies that can strengthen the U.S. competitive position. Actions should be taken to stimulate the formation of science parks, technology centers, and other forms of university-industry interaction. Antitrust laws should be relaxed at least enough to permit more corporate R&D collaboration. Specialized support should be provided to monitor worldwide technical developments and to increase the access of small firms to the latest technologies. Finally, managerial training at every level, from business schools to in-house development, must emphasize the importance of engineering, manufacturing, productivity, and innovation to overall long-range business success.

In short, America's initiative represents one of the greatest assets in our claim to international leadership in the next century. We are especially strong in entrepreneurship and could be as strong in technology by making some critical adjustments. It is important to place a high priority on preserving and extending our ability and will to exercise this kind of initiative in the future.

MASTERY OF INTERDEPENDENCE

With nations interconnected politically, economically, and electronically, international cooperation has become mandatory. The number of influential players on the world scene is multiplying, including not only nations but multinational corporations and bankers, international unions and other interest groups, international agencies such as the United Nations and the World Bank, and common markets and other entities created by treaties. Less can be done unilaterally. Even a policy that appears to be strictly domestic often has unexpected spillover effects on other nations.

For America to retain a leadership position among nations, this interdependence will have to be recognized much more than is currently realized. America has lagged behind most other nations in its international consciousness. Few

Americans are able to communicate in other languages. Marketers are often reluctant to seek out and accommodate the tastes and preferences of foreigners. Americans know far less about the people, governments, and customs of other lands than foreigners know about us.

Many other obstacles impede international cooperation. National sovereignty is still jealously guarded all over the world, and national loyalty is highly regarded everywhere. Accepted legal and behavioral norms differ in all the world's cultures, leading to frequent disagreement over methods, desired outcomes, and the distribution of costs and benefits. In the absence of international enforcement mechanisms, agreements depend either on goodwill and trust or on the threat of retaliation, neither of which provides complete assurance that the agreements will be observed.

Still, opportunities abound for American leadership because many kinds of cooperation are possible, as suggested in the following list presented at a top-level meeting of the Organization for Economic Cooperation and Development:

1. Exchange of information on the current situation and on current national policies. This form of cooperation is designed to assure the same information base, so to speak, and to avoid misunderstandings about what any country's policy actually is;

2. Agreement on common definitions of concepts and measurements, so all parties are reasonably confident that they are talking about the same thing;

3. Agreement on norms or objectives so all parties are assured that certain of their actions are aimed in the same direction, at shared if not completely common objectives;

4. Exchange of information on prospective policy actions, so that each party is not caught unawares by the actions of others and can prepare its own

actions to offset unwelcome side effects or to pursue
the same objective in parallel action;

5. Coordination of national actions, so that the various parties work in prearranged concert in the
pursuit of common objectives;

6. Joint action, in which actions are decided together
and taken together in the name of all participating
parties, and often involve joint expenditure with
shared contributions.

America is no novice at international agreements, of
course. We have some of the most skilled diplomats, experts,
and scholars in international relations in the world. We
have been a leader in the formation of many collaborative
efforts including the United Nations, NATO, OECD, and
many other agencies. For the most part, we have observed
our agreements, although there have been notable recent
exceptions such as the failure to pay our bills at the United
Nations or to recognize the authority of the International
Court of Justice when it is inconvenient for us to do so. Still,
there is much we can do to enhance our ability to master
international interdependence.

Just as the Europeans have linked neighboring economies to achieve the benefits of larger markets and a broader
base of innovation, so should the United States increase its
ties to its neighbors, especially Mexico. For example, the
nearly one thousand "maquiladora" assembly plants along
the U.S.-Mexican border employ some 310,000 Mexicans.
They help us lower the attractiveness of Asian imports
while retaining American design and manufacturing jobs
that might otherwise go overseas. They increase the economic viability and stability of Mexico, enabling it to pay
back its loans to American banks and to grow as an important market for American goods. Moreover, the collaboration of Mexican workers with American technical skills
may well produce items for export to third countries that

are more competitive with Asian products than either country could achieve on its own. With political problems in Central America, few countries may be more important to America's future than Mexico.

We have another great and often overlooked asset for mastering interdependence; we are blessed with the largest, most vibrant immigrant population in the world. Major cities like Los Angeles and New York are truly world cities, with dozens of ethnic enclaves providing faithful reproductions of foreign cultures and languages—Chinatown, Koreatown, Little Tokyo, and so on.

These ethnic enclaves are full of first- and second-generation ethnic Americans with great energy and confidence in the future of America. They provide a vivid example to the whole world of peaceful collaboration across cultures. They are natural bridges to foreign countries and, even more important, they provide living laboratories close to home for educating American citizens about foreign cultures and languages. The ethnic diversity of America, unmatched anywhere in the world, is an underappreciated asset in helping America master interdependence with other countries. We have only to learn how to use it more effectively.

NATIONAL INTEGRITY

Some people would argue that the term *national integrity* is an oxymoron. No sovereign nation has a spotless record of integrity, including the United States, with its history of breaking faith on Indian treaties, unfairly detaining Japanese-Americans in World War II, and denying rights to women and minorities.

All the same, as the world becomes more interdependent and collaborative, national integrity becomes more important as a foundation for joint action and trust. If America is to continue to be an international leader under these conditions, it will have to provide an example of national integrity that could serve as a model for others.

What are some of the necessary dimensions of national integrity? In the absence of any accepted definition, the following is offered as a starter list:

1. Respect for human life and the realization of human potential. National integrity demands respect for cultural diversity; universal human freedom; the elimination of illiteracy, ignorance, and other obstacles to the realization of full human dignity; and the development of all nations to their fullest potential.

2. Honesty. National integrity must be based on complete trustworthiness, including full compliance with all agreements and treaties, and international relations based on fair disclosure of truthful information.

3. Commitment to the global good. National integrity includes sharing and stewardship of the earth's resources and environments; a firm belief in universal progress; and a willingness to collaborate with all nations in the search for joint solutions to global problems.

4. Respect for the law. National integrity must be based on the rule of law, especially involving the use of rational discourse and agreed-on standards for the resolution of conflicts.

5. Equity. National integrity implies fair treatment of all parties and nations, social justice, mutual respect, and human decency in all interactions.

These are high standards, to be sure, but necessary for a nation to lead. America's score on these standards is better than that of many nations, but there is room for improvement. An important start could be made by empowering a commission to hold hearings and develop a statement of principles for U.S. conduct in relation to other nations, disseminating the results, and then enforcing compliance at the highest levels. This is also a proper subject for discussion and debate in schools and universities.

FINDING OUR WAY

A review of the characteristics of international leadership in the twenty-first century suggests that America is still very much in the running. We have major assets, including military and economic strength, an evolving distinctive competence in four areas critical to the future of civilization, an outstanding entrepreneurial capability, vibrant ethnic enclaves that provide laboratories for leadership, and some of the skills and elements of integrity most needed for international leadership.

We also have some major liabilities, including a lack of national vision and foresight, absence of national planning for transitions from military to economic investments, erosion of key technological advantages, and, worst of all, a seriously deteriorating education system that promises to put America at a perilous global disadvantage if not given the highest priority and massive investments in the coming decade.

The great basis for optimism about America's global leadership in the future is the fact that our assets are unmatched by any other nation, while all our liabilities are within our power to correct. None of them requires actions by others, and all of them are well within our own resources to accomplish.

America need not be a nation with a great future behind it. It can lead the world in the twenty-first century, but only if a conscious choice and commitment is made right now. In another ten years it may be too late, for there will have been further erosion of American competitiveness and perhaps irreparable harm to the learning potential of an entire generation.

We are truly at a crossroads. Ross Perot, an innovative and successful business leader, has the following quotation hanging on his office wall: "Every good and excellent thing stands moment by moment on the razor's edge of danger and must be fought for."

Will we fight for America's leadership?

12

EARNING THE RIGHT TO LEAD

*"We didn't inherit the land from our fathers,
we are borrowing it from our children."*

—Old Amish saying

NO ONE—NO person, no organization, and certainly no country—is born with the right to lead. Indeed, no one even deserves special consideration as a potential leader. Leadership is available to anyone with reasonable intelligence and drive, but it must be earned. The leader must pay the dues.

This book has described the seven megaskills of a new age of leadership in America. Those who aspire to leadership can earn the right to lead the old-fashioned way—by hard work to master and demonstrate the ability to apply the seven megaskills. But one other element is part of the admission price to leadership status, and that element—trusteeship for the future—is the subject of this final chapter.

WHO SPEAKS FOR THE FUTURE?

Americans have a great tradition of concern for the future that originates with the founding fathers. As they designed the engines of governance—the political parties, separation of church and state, an independent judiciary, the balance of powers, the Bill of Rights, and all the rest—they were keenly aware that they were making decisions for the sake of future generations. In one of George Washington's speeches, the term *posterity* was used nine times; subsequent statesmen were equally fond of the term. When did it go out of fashion?

Sometimes it seems as though this is the generation that killed posterity. Decisions are made with seemingly reckless unconcern about their future consequences. Some might protest that this generation, like all prior American generations, has a great sense of obligation to the future, that they love their children and want to pass on to them a better world than they found. But if we put aside this pious pleading and instead look coldly at what Americans are actually doing to future generations, we see quite a different picture. As the prior chapters have shown, our actions seem not only inconsiderate of future generations but downright antagonistic. For example:

▷We are loading our children up with debt, for which the interest and principal will have a substantial prior claim on a part of their income for their entire lives. Meanwhile, we use these borrowings for consumption rather than investing them in existing and new industries to create future growth.

▷We are allowing our environment to deteriorate recklessly, adding long-lasting poisons to air and water, depleting the ozone layer, losing valuable topsoil and forest lands, and allowing species to become extinct.

▷We are starving the school system, subjecting our children to an education totally inadequate for the challenges they will face, and inferior to that in the countries with which they will have to compete for employment and resources. Instead, by the time they're eighteen, our children will have spent, on average, fifteen thousand hours staring at television programs that, like visual junk food, provide little intellectual nourishment.

▷We are neglecting our infrastructure, leaving a legacy of rusting bridges, potholed roads, overloaded sewer systems, obsolete railroads, dangerously crowded airports, gridlocked cities, and inadequate or nonexistent public transportation systems.

▷We are allowing poverty and homelessness to continue, condemning as much as one-third of our youngsters to a childhood characterized by despair, hunger, abuse, or neglect, which diminishes their prospects for mastering the skills needed in the next century.

▷We provide bad ethical models for our kids, for almost daily they see stories of government corruption and private greed. Their heroes—football players, rock stars, corporate raiders, and all the rest—make it less likely that they will be guided by community values and respect for public institutions when they reach positions of influence.

▷We are stingy in making social investments in children even when an economically compelling argument can be made for doing so. For example, according to the House Select Committee on Children, Youth and Families, $1.00 in preschool education saves $4.75 in special education, welfare, and prison costs, and $1.00 in remedial education saves $6.00 in the cost of repeating a grade.

With this kind of a record, it is hard to make the case that current leaders care very much about generations to come. Children, of course, sense this, as even cursory attention to the lyrics of their popular tunes will attest. Is it surprising, then, that youngsters are "freaking out" with all sorts of maladaptive behavior—drugs, dropouts, suicides, teen pregnancy, date rape, gang wars, and the like? They seem to be crying out to the grown-ups, "Dear parents (if you are still our parents), stop polluting our future (if we still have a future)."

But who cares? Does the future really matter? As someone once said, "What has posterity ever done for me?" The answer is that it matters very much.

- It matters because concern for the future is the only way we can ever repay the incredible debt we owe to our own ancestors for making all the sacrifices and investments that have brought about our current state of comfort.

- It matters because we see ourselves as moral creatures who believe in the Golden Rule and, therefore, must treat our children and grandchildren as we ourselves would like to be treated were our roles reversed.

- It matters because we value the human species and American traditions and wish them to continue.

- It matters because, as human beings, we cannot bear to live a purposeless existence and would despair to think we had a hand in destroying or diminishing the only world we know to be capable of sustaining humankind.

- It matters because we are curious about the meaning of life and know it can be found only in the accumulation of knowledge and understanding over many generations.

- It matters because our religious beliefs compel us to leave the world a better place than we found it.

- And if none of these arguments prevail, it matters because, when we act to preserve and improve the future, we improve our own lives for whatever time remains to us.

Because the future truly matters, the second key to earning the right to lead must be a sense of trusteeship or stewardship toward the future. The answer to the question, "Who speaks for posterity?" is that the leader does. The leader not only is the ombudsman for the future but also the instrument we have designed for articulating our dreams, pointing the way toward their achievement, and helping us work with each other to create the future.

A person, social movement, organization, or country may possess all the megaskills, but if it can't demonstrate a powerful sense of responsibility for the collective future, it does not merit and will not receive the trust or commitment that alone will enable it to exercise leadership. If this sets a high standard for leadership, then it is about time. We have been expecting—and getting—too little from our leaders. The stakes are much too high to allow this to continue.

TOWARD A RENAISSANCE OF LEADERSHIP

I said in the first chapter that Americans perceive a leadership void that puts at risk our traditions, our livelihoods, our lifestyles, our future, and almost everything else we value. A new age of leadership is essential, worthwhile, and achievable. This book has examined what is expected of leaders and would-be leaders in earning the right to lead. Other institutions also have plenty to do if such a renaissance of American leadership is to be accomplished.

The education system faces perhaps the greatest challenge. Traditional responsibilities of educating for careers and citizenship must now be extended, adding education for futures-creative leadership. Young people must be taught what leadership is, why it is so important, and why they should aspire to become leaders. At the moment, students learn far more about leadership on television and movie screens than they do in classrooms, so it shouldn't be surprising if many of them view leaders as little more than charismatic manipulators pursuing selfish power goals, rather than as the very key to the effectiveness and viability of American institutions.

The schools can do much to promote leadership by creating new opportunities for student leaders both on and off campus. Already schools and universities offer leadership roles in sports, student government, clubs, publications, and fraternities and sororities. These are very good, and more such situations should be created, but they are only a first approximation of what leadership is really like. Other opportunities should be offered that would give students a more accurate experience in leadership roles. For example, helping students start small entrepreneurial ventures or form grass-roots political action groups around local environmental or social issues would give them a real taste of futures-creative leadership at its best.

Far from being peripheral to more traditional learning pursuits, these leadership experiences should be highly valued in themselves. They should be further enhanced by counseling, mentoring, and peer group discussions on how to improve student leadership skills and increase confidence in them. A reasonable goal would be at least one or two leadership experiences during each student's educational career.

Nor should the classroom be overlooked as a place for learning to lead. Among the subjects that should be covered as a part of already-existing courses are the history and philosophy of leadership, interpersonal skills, the lives of great leaders, leadership strategies, international relations, and ethics. It is especially important that prospective leaders learn how to think about change and complexity and how to anticipate future developments in such areas as technology, demographics, and social values.

The classroom should be linked more effectively to real-life leadership experiences: guest lecturers chosen from among successful leaders in public and private organizations; field visits to their offices and facilities; and writing assignments on case studies of successful leadership. Feedback on leadership progress and potential should also be provided to every student, with prizes for exceptional achievement.

Improving the leadership orientation of schools and universities must start with the teaching staff. Unfortunately, few teachers or college faculty know much about leadership, and the subject crosses traditional departmental disciplines. Administrators need to give high priority to this subject and support efforts to improve the faculty's ability to recognize, motivate, and enhance leadership skills.

But the schools can't do it all. Families need to provide a suitable environment within which young leaders can be nurtured and encouraged. Children should be gently urged to "go for it," to seek leadership challenges at every stage of their development. Particular care should be taken to see that they learn how to work well together in groups. Home is the place to develop that critical sense of personal and group integrity. Youngsters can be made to understand at an early age that they have it in their ability to change the world for the better, and they should aspire to do no less.

The media also have an important role to play in making leadership more attractive, appreciated, and understood. The media should exercise much more responsibility in whom and what they choose to celebrate and applaud. A corporate raider who gets rich while laying off hundreds and impoverishing whole communities should not get the same media respect and attention as a successful entrepreneur who has built a business or created a new niche in the international marketplace. The head of a government agency who cleans up some part of the environment deserves at least as much attention as currently accorded a government official who has breached the public trust. Stereotypes, such as the well-meaning but bumbling police chief, and news broadcasts that give political leaders thirty seconds to explain complicated social issues, do not increase respect for leadership.

Instead, leaders should be depicted more accurately in terms of what they do, what they care about, and what they wish for their organizations and the nation. There should be prime-time programs on successful leaders, past and present, depicting their challenges, lifestyles, and accomplishments. During a presidential election the media should broadcast critical analyses of the candidates' leadership track records, as well as expert opinions on what leadership skills and experiences are most needed to address the issues likely to arise during the winner's term of office. And certainly, programs for children should not be offered without a keen sense of responsibility for how they are shaping future minds, attitudes, and aspirations.

Organizations also have responsibilities for improving the quality of leadership in America. A large corporation like General Electric, or a large public agency, hospital, school system, or other group, can create thousands of leadership roles at every level in the organization. Undoubtedly, an organization of this size already has hundreds, perhaps thousands, of employees with extraordinary leadership skills, many of whom do not get much chance to prove their abilities at work. Instead, they use their spare time to head PTAs, church groups, or Little League teams.

A large organization should encourage such activities, of course, but also should consciously create programs to further develop and apply these abilities to its own problems. This requires leadership-oriented job rotation programs, as well as specially designed leadership development programs. Much of what passes for leadership training in such organizations at the moment is really management development, which is more concerned with efficient operations than discovering new directions for the future.

Finally, a renaissance of American leadership will require millions of Americans to stand up and take personal responsibility for the future of this country. In the past several decades, entitlement programs have grown rapidly without a concomitant sense of responsibility to the nation or organization that is providing the benefits. Entitlements do not produce the good life; effort and commitment do. In the long run, this nation and its institutions can assume leadership roles in the world only if its people are willing to do so. That is the final element in earning the right to lead.

The great gift of the leader is to enable us to see what we should aspire to and what we can become, individually and collectively, and to show us how to do it. There is nothing America needs more at this moment than a true renaissance of leadership at every level.

It is within our grasp. We may not get another chance.

APPENDIX:
THE QUEST FOR
STRATEGIC PLANNING*

QUEST (QUICK ENVIRONMENTAL Scanning Technique) is general enough to be useful in virtually any organization no matter how large or small—provided only that management is committed to strategic thinking. I have used QUEST successfully at seven large corporations and at half a dozen governmental, educational, and nonprofit agencies. The success of the method is attested to by the enthusiasm of those who have used it. Recently I ran into a corporate CEO, and I asked him about the aftermath of a QUEST we had undertaken in his firm four years earlier. He replied: "We're still living off the intellectual capital we created during that exercise."

The QUEST process involves two full-day meetings (usually separated by about a month) of a group of twelve to eighteen managers. At the first meeting, participants examine the environment of the corporation for the next five to twenty years to identify major threats and opportunities.

* Article by Burt Nanus adapted and reprinted with permission from *New Management* 2:1, 1984, 58–61.

Between the sessions, these findings are analyzed and several future scenarios are developed. At the second session, the participants identify and prioritize the issues that arise out of the scenarios, and identify strategic options to deal with the issues that have been surfaced.

DOES THE "BIG MAC" HAVE A FUTURE?

Let me illustrate the QUEST process with a hypothetical example. Assume you are part of the management team of a chain of restaurants. Almost certainly you would have a marketing strategy that positions your restaurants in one of the major market niches—self-service or full-service, youth-oriented or adult-oriented, eat-in or take-out, sophisticated or simple foods, price-sensitive or quality-sensitive. At the same time, you would be concerned about developments that might impact this strategy, such as changes in consumer tastes and attitudes, government regulation, the technology of food preparation, energy costs, competitive strategies, and even new medical findings about nutrition and health. You would want to develop an understanding of what changes might occur, what they would mean, and how they might affect the restaurant industry. And you would want to look for a set of strategies that would help your restaurant chain succeed given any of these changes that might occur.

How do you start this quest? With QUEST. You bring together your group of managers and begin by delimiting the boundaries of the inquiry. For example, your group of managers might conclude that any major strategic decision, such as opening new types of restaurants or moving into new geographic areas, would take years to implement. So it makes sense to focus on the 1988 to 2000 time frame. They might further agree to limit their discussion to changes that directly affect the restaurant chain and its immediate stakeholders—for example, customers, employees, stockholders, competitors, local government, food distributors and suppliers, food manufacturers. Each member of the group would nominate the five most important stakeholders from such a list (measured by the degree to which the stakeholder affects or is affected by the restaurant chain). Your group would then list their assumptions about what these few key stakeholders will seek from the corporation in the future. For example, it might be assumed that customers will seek value, nutrition, good taste, variety, safety, ambience, consistency, convenience, and good service.

The discussion would then turn to measures of the restaurant chain's performance. Here's a question that would focus the discussion: "If you were to come back in twenty years and wanted to evaluate the success of our chain over the intervening years, what measures would you inquire about?" In response to this question, the group might propose such measures as profitability, efficiency, financial risk, the state of employee relationships, customer satisfaction, market share, image, and service excellence. Again, the group would rank order the list and pick the five most important measures. (These will be used at a later stage in evaluating the various strategic options available to the corporation.)

The discussion to this point will have taken about two hours. Now the participants would focus their attention on critical events that could happen between this year and the year 2000 which, if they did occur, would greatly affect the organization's viability. First the group might think of developments that would affect customer needs and wants. Then they might explore developments in such areas as raw materials, energy, technology, capital, facilities, equipment, regulatory changes, competitive changes, and human resources. In three hours or so, it would not be at all difficult for the group to identify 150 to 200 such developments. Some examples of developments that might be identified are listed in the accompanying box.

POSSIBLE FUTURE DEVELOPMENTS THAT COULD AFFECT THE RESTAURANT BUSINESS

- More working women in the population have less time to prepare food at home
- The discovery of new protein sources that do not involve meat
- Development of more sophisticated tastes (ethnic foods, health foods, lighter foods)
- Very high nutrition consciousness
- Much higher food costs
- High cost energy
- Disruption of some food supplies due to political unrest
- Great expansion of fast-food outlets
- More restaurants in retail stores
- Cheaper, novel packaging for raw foodstuffs
- New preservation methods for foods
- High cost of capital for investment
- Environmental restrictions on restaurant operations
- Use of robots in restaurant kitchens
- "Truth in menu" regulations
- Doubling of the minimum wage
- Large consumer companies entering the restaurant business
- Professionalization of restaurant management
- Government-sponsored communal kitchens for senior citizens

Next, the group would prioritize these developments. Each participant would have, say, ten votes to select the changes that would have the greatest impact on the restaurant chain (were they to occur). The group would attempt to narrow the list to the ten or fifteen major developments most likely to influence strategic decisions. The group would then reformulate these major events to make them precise. For example:

- "High food costs" becomes "The real cost of raw food-stuffs at least doubles by the year 2000."

- "High energy costs" becomes "The real costs of gasoline and oil triple by the year 2000."

- "Expansion of fast food" becomes "Fast-food chains become more than 50 percent of the restaurant industry by the year 2000."

The group would then engage in a simplified "Delphi" process to determine the probabilities of each of these major events. For example, each participant would write down a probability estimate for each event ranging from zero (if the event is seen as impossible), to 50 percent (if it is as likely as not to occur), to 100 percent (if it is certain to occur by the year 2000). These estimates are then collected and displayed to the group. On items on which there is no consensus, a discussion would ensue in which those who are at the high or low ends of the distribution would offer reasons for their estimates. After the discussion, there would be a second round of estimation. (Two rounds are usually enough to obtain some sense of convergence on a median probability.)

This process of probability estimation is very important. Since all of the events on the short list were previously judged to have a high impact on the restaurant business, those that also have a high probability of occurrence demand immediate strategy attention. (Events having lower probabilities of occurrence would require systematic monitoring and reevaluation over time.)

The next step would be for each participant to fill out a simple "cross-impact matrix" relating each of the major events to each of the others. A person who is totally unfamiliar with cross-impact procedures will spend approximately forty-five minutes completing a matrix that contains twelve events. In the process of filling out the matrix, he or she will have created a mental model of how the world is expected to work in the future, and how these critical developments relate to the firm's business.

The cross-impact analysis is useful because it shows which events are *driving forces*—that is, those that greatly change the probability of the occurrence of other events. It also shows which are the important *reactor events*—those that are driven by other developments. While a reactor may have a low probability of occurrence, its probability will be greatly increased if certain other events occur—and such relationships are important to understand. Beyond, it is possible to use cross-impact analysis to reveal areas of disagreement among the participants about the effects of important developments, and to understand which events tend to cluster in patterns of mutual cause and effect.

But all that would happen in the next phase. For now, the day's activities would come to a close. As we see, the discussion during this first day has been about major dimensions of change that could impact the restaurant chain, with full scope given for creative exploration by the group. Quite aside from the specific information generated about future environments, when properly conducted such a session can be very intense, stimulating, and intellectually productive for the participants.

HOMEWORK BETWEEN THE MEETINGS

As the first session progressed, the data developed will have been captured by a facilitator on flip charts and on the cross-impact forms. Based on these materials, a report is then prepared that depicts and analyzes the external environment of the restaurant chain. In addition to being a record of what transpired at the first meeting, the report would include scenarios developed from the entire list of events identified by the participants, and from an analysis of the cross-impact model. These scenarios might be distinguished by the major forces that shape the future of the restaurant chain. For example, the various scenarios might be titled: "Business as Usual," "Energy Driven," "Food-Price Driven," "Technology Driven," or "Government Driven." The "Business as Usual Scenario" might describe how the environment would evolve from the current momentum of society, given the events the participants considered most likely to occur. The "Energy Driven Scenario" might then superimpose very high energy prices and some energy scarcity on the first scenario. A "Government Driven Scenario" would be characterized by greatly increased government regulation of the restaurant industry. And so on. Each of the scenarios would be designed to be distinctly different from the others, internally consistent, plausible, and sufficiently detailed to be useful in the next stage of the process.

THE SECOND MEETING

The second meeting would take place approximately a month after the first. The session would start with a discussion of the contents of the report (permitting the participants to present any new insights they may have had since the last meeting), followed by their comments regarding the completeness and relevance of the trends and events they identified, and their interpretation of the conclusions about the external environment.

After this general discussion, the participants would examine each of the scenarios from the point of view of the current strategy of the restaurant chain. They would list the potential strengths and weaknesses of the corporation in dealing with each scenario. Strengths might involve the chain's current location, reputation, quality of management, customer image, and ability to attract financial resources. Weaknesses might include difficulties in recruiting competent staff or high leasing costs relative to competitors. The group then can identify key issues that arise under many different scenarios. These may include issues of competitive strength, efficiency, response to market changes, financial concerns, production processes, or similar considerations. Now they are cooking!

The group then turns to the major purpose of the second meeting: identifying the strategic options that are available given the full range of events they have analyzed. Prior to the meeting, a series of categories would have been chosen within which these strategic options might be listed such as marketing options, mergers and joint ventures, resource acquisition options, efficiency-enhancing options. Under "marketing options," the group might consider strategic alternatives with regard to price, service, and expansion into new markets. Under "mergers and joint ventures," the group might consider buying a small chain of taco stands or entering into a joint venture with a department store chain. Within two to three hours, the group could identify more than a hundred such strategic options. If the session must end after half a day, the meeting could be closed with a vote designed to narrow the set of strategic options to the best five to ten. At this point, the corporation president might step in and assign individual responsibility for analyzing each of these strategic options, perhaps asking these individuals to assemble a small team to develop recommendations.

If the group can spend the remainder of the day in the meetings, they would go on to examine the high priority strategies with regard to their risks and rewards, resource requirements, and impact upon stakeholders.

BENEFITS OF THE QUEST APPROACH

The most important benefit of this approach is a new sense of shared understanding of the organization's external environment. After a QUEST exercise, participants will often remark how it clarified their thinking about the future. For some, there is a sense of discovery or insight into issues that previously had appeared vague or only dimly perceived. For others, there is a shift in perception or a clarification of opposing views.

The process is systemic and comprehensive, while at the same time open to divergent opinions. It allows for wide-ranging speculation without being threatening to any of the participants. More important, it helps the participants converge on an action agenda. All of this tends to facilitate subsequent implementation, and to provide guidance to the formal strategic planning process. As a result, an appetite is created for more detailed and thorough analyses of future environments.

Of course, this process (or any process of a similar sort) has no inherent magic. The results will only be as good as the participants themselves and, therefore, will suffer from inbreeding, dominance of conventional wisdom, or failure of imagination or nerve. The process often illuminates where understanding is weak and where additional insight is required. However, at the very least, the group consensus will be documented and can then be tested against outside views. At best, you might just come up with a strategy to rival Ray Kroc's or Colonel Sanders's!

NOTES

CHAPTER 1
AMERICA OUT OF FOCUS

Page 3. The quotation from Louis Harris appears in *Inside America* by Louis Harris (New York: Vintage Books, 1987), page 123.

Page 3. The *USA Today* survey results appear in *USA Today: Tracking Tomorrow's Trends* by Anthony M. Casale (Kansas City: Andrews, McMeel and Parker, 1986), page 202.

Page 6. The earlier book referred to is *Leaders: The Strategies for Taking Charge*, by Warren Bennis and Burt Nanus (New York: Harper and Row, 1985).

CHAPTER 2
THE CHALLENGE TO LEADERSHIP

Page 14. The data comparing U.S. to foreign per capita gross domestic product is from *Statistical Abstract of the United States—1988* (Washington, D.C.: U.S. Government Printing Office, 1987), page 419.

Page 14. The data on foreign ownership of U.S. assets are from "The Selling of America" by Jaclyn Fierman, *Fortune*, May 23, 1988, pages 54 and 55.

Page 14. The productivity figures appeared in "Losing the Lead," the *Wall Street Journal*, October 24, 1988, page A1.

Page 15. The one hundred largest public companies were listed in *Business Week*, July 18, 1988, page 138, and the largest banking firms were listed in *Business Week*, June 27, 1988, page 76.

Page 16. The political poll quotation is from *Inside America* by Louis Harris (New York: Vintage Books, 1987), page 338.

Page 18. The statement on the role of work appears in *Habits of the Heart* by Robert N. Bellah, et al. (New York: Perennial Library, 1985), page 66.

Page 21. The Conference Board estimate is from "In Increasing Numbers, White Collar Workers Leave Steady Positions" by Michael McCarthy, the *Wall Street Journal,* October 13, 1987, page 1.

Page 21. The *USA Today* poll is reported in *USA Today: Tracking Tomorrow's Trends* by Anthony M. Casale (Kansas City: Andrews, McMeel and Parker, 1986), page 108.

Page 22. The data on alienation and unhappiness are from *Inside America* by Louis Harris, (New York: Vintage Books, 1987), pages 125 and 126.

Page 22. The quotation by Woody Allen is from *Side Effects* by Woody Allen (New York: Random House, 1975), page 57.

CHAPTER 3
THE NEW AGE

Page 32. The quotation is from *The Emerging Network Marketplace* by Herbert S. Dordick, Helen G. Bradley, and Burt Nanus (Norwood, New Jersey: Ablex Publishing Company, 1981), pages 6 and 7. Reprinted by permission of the publisher.

Page 37. The quotation is from "America's New Geostrategy" by Zbigniew Brzezinski, *Foreign Affairs,* 66:4, Spring 1988, page 694.

Page 40. The quotation is from "The Triumph of Technology: 'Can' Implies 'Ought' " by Hasan Ozbekhan in *Planning for Diversity and Choice,* edited by Stanford Anderson (Cambridge, Massachusetts: MIT Press, 1968), page 205.

Page 41. The quotation by Tom Peters is from *Thriving on Chaos* (New York: Alfred A. Knopf, Inc., 1987), page 45.

Page 43. The quotation is from *Winnie-the-Pooh* by A. A. Milne (New York: E. P. Dutton & Co., Inc., 1926), page 3.

CHAPTER 4
LEADERSHIP MATTERS

Page 45. The quotation is from *Human Betterment* by Kenneth E. Boulding (Beverly Hills, California: Sage Publications, 1985), page 74.

Page 46. The quotation is from *The Functions of the Executive* by Chester I. Barnard (Cambridge, Massachusetts: Harvard University Press, 1962 edition of original 1938 book), page 283.

Page 47–51. The discussion on leadership summarizes the message of the author's prior book, *Leaders: The Strategies for Taking Charge* by Warren Bennis and Burt Nanus (New York: Harper and Row, 1985). Adapted from *Leaders: The Strategies for Taking Charge* by Warren Bennis and Burt Nanus. Copyright © 1985 Warren Bennis and Burt Nanus. By permission of Harper & Row, Publishers, Inc.

Page 51. The quotation is from *Leadership* by James MacGregor Burns (New York: Harper and Row, 1978), page 439.

CHAPTER 5
FUTURES-CREATIVE LEADERSHIP

Page 61. The quotation is from *The Art of Conjecture* by Bertrand deJouvenel (New York: Basic Books, Inc., 1967), page 19.
Page 65. The quotation is from *Freedom in a Rocking Boat* by Sir Geoffrey Vickers (London: The Penguin Press, 1970), page 96.

CHAPTER 6
LEADERSHIP ROLES

Page 71. The quotation is from *Children of Dune* by Frank Herbert (New York: Berkley Publishing, 1976), page 360.
Page 72. The quotation by Louis Madelin appears in *Napoleon*, edited by Maurice Hutt (Englewood Cliffs, New Jersey: Prentice-Hall, 1972), page 151.
Page 72. The quotations from Napoleon appear in *The Mind of Napoleon* by J. Christopher Herold (New York: Columbia University Press, 1955), pages 164 and 169.
Page 73. The quotation by McHale is from *The Future of the Future* by John McHale (New York: George Braziller, 1969), page 9.
Page 73. The quotation by deBono is from *Tactics—The Art and Science of Success* by Edward deBono (New York: Little, Brown and Company, 1984), page 4.
Page 73. The statement by Ronald Reagan was made at the Moscow Summit, May 31, 1988.

CHAPTER 7
THE SEVEN MEGASKILLS

Page 81. The article referred to is "The Seven Keys to Business Leadership" by Kenneth Labich, *Fortune*, October 24, 1988, pages 58–66.
Page 82. The quotation by Peter Brook is from "Peter Brook Creates a Nine Hour Epic" by Margaret Croyden, the *New York Times Magazine*, October 4, 1987, page 40. Copyright © 1987 by The New York Times Company. Reprinted by permission.
Page 94. The quotation from Dean Tjosvold is from *Working Together to Get Things Done* by Dean Tjosvold (Lexington, Massachusetts: Heath and Company, 1986), page 25.
Page 95. The quotation by Jim Robinson is from "Do You Know Me?" by Anthony Bianco in *Business Week*, January 25, 1988, page 76.
Page 96. The quotations from Dag Hammarskjöld are from *Markings* by Dag Hammarskjöld (New York: Alfred A. Knopf, 1966), pages 65, 84, 105, 111, and 156.

CHAPTER 8
THE LEADER'S EDGE

Page 100. The Center for Creative Leadership studies are reported in *The Lessons of Experience* by Morgan W. McCall, Jr., Michael M. Lombardo, and Ann M. Morrison (Lexington, Massachusetts: Lexington Books, 1988).

Page 101. The quotation is from *The Chosen* by Chaim Potok (New York: Fawcett Press, 1967), page 114.

Page 101. The quotation is from "The Mystery of the Business Leader" by Peter Drucker, the *Wall Street Journal*, September 29, 1987, page 28. Reprinted with the permission of the *Wall Street Journal* copyright © 1989 Dow Jones & Company, Inc. All rights reserved.

Page 102. The values studies were reported in "Nature or Nurture? Study Blames Ethical Lapses on Corporate Goals" by Rick Wartzman, the *Wall Street Journal*, October 9, 1987, page 27.

Page 105. The quotation is from *The Book of Abraham* by Marek Halter, translated by Lowell Bair, page 185. Copyright © 1983 by Editions Robert Laffont, S. A. Translation copyright © 1986 by Henry Holt & Company. Reprinted by permission of Henry Holt and Company, Inc.

Page 107. Excerpt from "Upon This Age, That Never Speaks Its Mind" by Edna St. Vincent Millay. From *Collected Poems* Harper & Row. Copyright © 1939, 1967 by Edna St. Vincent Millay and Norma Millay Ellis. Reprinted by permission.

Page 121. The quotation is from "Management from Within" by Ray Bradbury, *New Management*, 1:4, 1984, page 15.

CHAPTER 9
BUILDING ORGANIZATIONAL CAPITAL

Page 138. The Southern California Edison strategic planning process is described in *Strategies for an Uncertain Future* (Los Angeles: Southern California Edison Company, March 1988).

CHAPTER 10
AMERICAN LEADERSHIP
IN THE TWENTY-FIRST CENTURY

Page 162. The quotation is from *The Next American Frontier* by Robert B. Reich (New York: Penguin Books, 1983), page 271.

CHAPTER 11
PERESTROIKA AMERICANA

Page 170. The statistics on energy efficiency are from "The Avoidable Oil Crisis" by Amory B. Lovins and L. Hunter Lovins, *The Atlantic*, December 1987, pages 22–29.

Page 172. The cost of cleaning up radioactive waste is estimated in "Radioactive Waste" by Robert Alvarez and Arjun Makhijani, *Technology Review*, August–September 1988, page 42.

Page 178. The data are from *USA Today: Tracking Tomorrow's Trends* by Anthony M. Casale (Kansas City: Andrews, McMeel and Parker, 1986), page 133.

Page 182. The data on patents are from *Statistical Abstract of the United States—1988* (Washington, D.C.: U.S. Government Printing Office, December 1987), page 518.

Page 183. The statistics on scientists and engineers are from "Economic Consequences of the Arms Race: The Second Rate Economy" by Seymour Melman, *The American Economic Review*, May 1988, page 56.

Page 185. The quotation is from "International Economic Cooperation: Overview and a Glimpse of the Future" by Richard N. Cooper, in *Interdependence and Cooperation in Tomorrow's World* (Paris, France: Organization for Economic Cooperation and Development, 1987), page 183.

Page 189. The sign on Ross Perot's wall was quoted in "The Irritant They Call Perot" by N. R. Kleinfield, the *New York Times*, April 27, 1986, Section 3, page 8.

CHAPTER 12
EARNING THE RIGHT TO LEAD

Page 193. The data from the House Select Committee on Children, Youth and Families was quoted in "What the Underclass Can't Get Out from Under," *Business Week*, September 19, 1988, page 123.

INDEX

Accelerator technologies, 30–31, 33

Acid rain, 35

Adams, John, 174

Allen, Woody, 22

Ambiguity, regarding intentions, 27–28

America. *See* United States

American Express Company, 64, 95

American Hospital Supply Corporation, 92–93

Andreas Stihl, 144

Anthony, Susan B., 6

Anticipatory learning, as leadership skill, 88–90, 97, 136–40, 173–78

Antitrust laws, 183, 184

Apple Computer, 6, 91

Arafat, Yassir, 74

Art of Conjecture, The (deJouvenel), 61

Atlantic Richfield, 134

Attention, management of, 49

Attributes, ranking of, 102

Auto industry, 179

Balanced growth, importance of, 147

Banking industry, 38, 179

Barnard, Chester I., 46

Bellah, Robert, 18

Bennis, Warren, 6, 47

Bhopal, 35

Biotechnology and health care, 169–70

Bjorklund, Glenn J., 138–40

Bonaparte, Napoleon, 55, 71–72

Boulding, Kenneth, 45

Bradbury, Ray, 121

Brain, unique feature of human, 59

Brook, Peter, 82–83

Brzezinski, Zbigniew, 37

Budget deficits, problem of, 2–3, 38

Burns, James MacGregor, 51

Capability, 102
Capitalism, 12
Carter, Jimmy, 75, 119, 157
Center for Creative Leadership,
    100
Change
    mastery of, as leadership
        skill, 84–87, 129–33,
        159–63
    role of values in management
        of, 64–65
Change agent, futures-creative
    leader as, 75–76
Charge, strategies for taking,
    49–50
Chernobyl, 35
Chosen, The, 101
Chrysler, 6, 77, 103
Churchill, Winston, 6, 55
Coach, futures-creative leader
    as, 77–78, 97
Coca-Cola, 130
Colgate Palmolive, 136
Commitment time, 128, 129
Communications, 27–28, 31
Communism, 12
Competence, building
    distinctive, 133–36
Computers, 31
    combination of, and
        telecommunications, 32
Conferencing, 179
Confidence, in institutions, 4, 5
Corporate leadership, 24–25
Corporations, restructuring of,
    39
Crown Books, 134
CSX Corporation, 27

deBono, 73
Deforestation, 35
deJouvenel, Bertrand, 61
Delphi technique, 109

Desertification, 35
Direction-setter, futures-
    creative leader as, 73–74
Direction-setting, importance
    of, in leadership, 73–74,
    156–57
Disney, Walt, 124, 130, 132
Distinctive competence,
    development of, 134
Downsizing, 19–20
Drucker, Peter, 101–2, 141

Eastman, George, 6
Eastman Kodak, 26
Economic renewal, 37–40,
    159–63
Education
    revitalization of, 173–78
    role of, in promoting
        leadership, 195–97
    selected statistics on
        American, 175
Eisenhower, Dwight D., 29–30,
    174
Electronic mail, 31, 179
Emerson, Ralph Waldo, 9
Empowerment, 51
Energy conservation, 170–72
Entrepreneurship, and
    innovation, 178–84
Environmental protection,
    172–73
Environmental threats, 17, 35
Ethical compliance, interest of
    futures-creative leader in,
    111–12
European Common Market,
    127
European Economic
    Community, 35
Exit interviews, 112
Experts, use of, by futures-
    creative leader, 109, 111

Families, two-income, 20–21

Family income, 15
Family life, as American value, 21
Family security, 102
Farsightedness, as leadership skill, 82–84, 97, 117, 124–29, 153–59
Flexibility, 129
  importance of, 115
Ford, Henry, 46
Ford Motor Company, 143–44
Forecasting, 65–66, 139
France, Anatole, 11
Freedom, 102
Friedan, Betty, 75
Fun, having, 119, 121
Future
  leaders as spokesmen for, 192–95
  role of leader in understanding, 58–66
  sources of information on, 63–64
Future-oriented organization, 124–29
  comparison of, to present-oriented organization, 130
  definition of, 127
Futures-creative leader(s), 54–70, 73–79, 124. *See also* Leader(s)
  anticipatory learning for, 88–90, 136–40, 173–78
  as change agent, 75–76
  as coach, 77–78, 97
  in designing robust strategies, 112–16
  and development of vision, 105–7
  as direction-setter, 73–74
  and ethical compliance, 111–12
  farsightedness of, 82–84, 124–29, 153–59

  importance of high moral standards for, 101–5
  importance of information to, 107–12
  initiative of, 90–93, 140–41, 178–84
  integrity standards of, 95–97, 145–47, 187–88
  interest of, in the future, 58–66, 111
  and mastery of change, 84–87, 129–33, 159–63
  and mastery of interdependence, 93–95, 97, 117, 142–44, 184–87
  and organization design, 87–88, 133–36, 166–78
  personal development of, 116–21
  personal philosophy for, 120
  as spokesperson, 76–77
  trend monitoring by, 108–9, 110
  use of experts by, 109, 111
Future Shock, 59
Futures Research Group, 158

Gandhi, Mahatma, 6, 116
General Electric, 135–36
General Foods, 136
General Motors, 20, 27, 92, 124, 132, 170
Genetic engineering, 31
Gielgud, John, 82
Global 2000 Report to the President, 157
Global connections, 33–37
Global imperative, 142–44
Global integration, 42
Global interdependence, 35
Global studies, sponsoring of long-range, 157–58
Goodyear Tire and Rubber, 129
Grant, Ulysses S., 174

Gross national product, in
U.S., 13-14

Hammarskjöld, Dag, 95-96
Harbison, Earle, Jr., 169
Harris, Louis, 3
Hazardous waste disposal, 35
Health care, and
biotechnology, 169-70
Hedging, 114-15
Heifetz, Jascha, 77
Herbert, Frank, 71
Herman, Woody, 95
Hitler, Adolph, 46
Holography techniques, 31
Honesty, 102
Housman, A. E., 55
Human capital, 130

Iacocca, Lee, 6, 52, 77, 103
IBM, 127
Information, sources of, on
future, 63-64
Information/communication
technologies and services,
167-68
Information Society, 31-32
Initiative, as leadership skill,
90-93, 140-41, 178-84
Innovation, and
entrepreneurship, 178-84
Institutional design
competence of U.S. in,
166-78
as leadership skill, 87-88,
133-36, 166-78
Institutions, confidence in, 4, 5
Integrity, as leadership skill,
95-97, 118, 145-47, 187-88
Intentions, ambiguity
regarding, 27-28
Interactive education, 32
Interdependence, mastery of, as
leadership skill, 93-95, 97,
117, 184-87, 142-44

International Association for
Evaluation of Educational
Achievement, 174
International competitiveness,
25
International leadership,
151-52

Job assignments, seeking
varied, 118
Jobs, Steve, 6, 54, 74
Johnson & Johnson, 134,
145-46, 179
Just-in-time delivery systems,
179

Kennedy, John F., 1, 68, 95,
116, 174
King, Martin Luther, 6, 54, 78,
116

Labor productivity, 19
Land, Edwin, 54, 75
Lao Tzu, 57
Laser techniques, 31
Layoffs, 20
Leader(s). *See also* Futures-
creative leader(s)
as change agent, 75-76
characteristics of, 8-9
comparison of managers
with, 6-7, 47-49
failure of, to recognize
important trends, 25-27
lessons for, 40-43
ranking of values and
attributes by, 102-3
as self-designed individuals,
99-100
strategies of, for taking
charge, 49-50
*Leaders: The Strategies for
Taking Charge* (Bennis and
Nanus), 6, 47
Leadership, 45-56

assessing quality of
  American, 11–12
challenges for, 11–28, 52–56
as culture-dependent, 46
definition of, 46–47
designing your jobs in, 119
developing extended model
  of, 66–70
earning right in, 191–99
effective, 7
and exercise power, 50–51
failures of, 23–28
as human characteristic,
  45–46
importance of, 45
inadequacies of, 66–67, 68
literature of, 47
megaskills of, 8–9, 81–98
need for, 7
new perspective on, 7–9
recognizing good, 46
requirements for successful,
  67
role of education in
  promoting, 195–97
role of media in promoting,
  197–98
role of organization, in
  promoting, 198–99
roles and skills in, 71–79
seeking responsibilities in,
  116
on state level, 23–24
styles of, 47
toward renaissance of,
  195–99
traits of, 47
understanding, 46–52
void in, 6–7
Leadership (Burns), 51
Leadership information
  systems, importance of, to
  futures-creative leader,
  107–12
Lead time, 128

Leisure time, 21–22
Levi Strauss, 103
Library services, 32
Lifestyle, 18
  role of, in self-realization,
    21–22
Lincoln, Abraham, 6, 55, 174
Lincoln Electric, 103
Lloyd George, David, 165
Longfellow, Henry Wadsworth,
  149
Los Angeles Lakers, 131

Machiavelli, 47
Madelin, Louis, 71–72
Managers, comparison of, with
  leaders, 6–7, 47–49
Manville Corporation, 146
Mao Tse-tung, 55
Markings (Hammarskjöld),
  95–96
Mastery of change, as
  leadership skill, 84–87,
  129–33, 159–63
Mastery of interdependence, as
  leadership skill, 93–95, 97,
  142–44, 184–87
Materials, new, 31
McCall, Morgan, 100
McHale, 73
Meaning, management of, 49
Media, role of, in promoting
  leadership, 197–98
Megaskills, 8, 81–82
  anticipatory learning, 88–90,
    97, 136–40, 173–78
  farsightedness, 82–84, 97,
    114, 124–29, 153–59
  initiative, 90–93, 140–41,
    178–84
  integrity standards, 95–97,
    118, 145–47, 187–88
  mastery of change, 84–87,
    129–33, 159–63
  mastery of interdependence,

93-95, 97, 142-44,
    184-87
organization design, 87-88,
    133-36, 166-78
Megatrends, 59
"Me Generation," 22
Mentor, leader as, 54, 116-17
Merck, 127
Microsoft, 64, 132
Military power, security
    through, 16-17
Millay, Edna St. Vincent, 107
Ministry of International Trade
    & Industry (MITI), 182
Mobil, 132
Models, 65-66
Moral standards, importance of
    high, 101-5
Moses, 55
MTM, 77
Multinational companies, 34
Musashi, Miyamoto, 29

National foresight, 153-59
National integrity, 187-88
Network information services,
    32-33
Next American Frontier, The
    (Reich), 162-63
NUMMI project, 92

Office automation, 32
Office of Technology
    Assessment (OTA), U.S.,
    156
Oil spills, 35
Olivetti, 144
Opinion polls, 112
Optimism, basis for, 1-2, 4,
    189
Organizational capital,
    building, 123-47
Organizational innovation,
    sparking, 140-41
Organizational integrity, as

leadership skill, 145-47
Organization design. *See*
    Institutional design
Organization for Economic
    Cooperation and
    Development, 185-86
Organizations, role of, in
    promoting leadership,
    198-99
O'Shaughnessy, Arthur, 99
Overfishing, 35
Ozbekhan, Hassan, 40-41
Ozone layer, depletion of, 35

Perestroika, 163
Perot, Ross, 189
Personal character, developing,
    118
Personal development, by
    futures-creative leaders,
    116-21
Personal leadership, 53-54
Personal relationships, role of,
    in self-realization, 21
Peters, Tom, 41, 141
Physical wealth, 130
Pierce, Nat, 95
Polaroid, 26, 124
Political persuasion, 173-74
Possible futures, 60-61
Posterity, 192
Preferable futures, 61
Prince, The (Machiavelli), 47
Probable futures, 61
Production facility, 32
Profiles in Courage (Kennedy),
    116
Prosperity, through economic
    growth, 12-16
Public policy, 13

Quaker Oats, 103
QUEST approach, 105, 109

Reagan, Ronald, 17, 73, 157

Red Cross, 130
Regulatory policy, 171
Reich, Robert, 162–63
Remote medical consultation,
    31–32
Research and development, 179,
    182–84
Researcher, thinking like,
    118–19
Responsibility, 102
Restructuring, 42
  economic renewal through,
    37–40
Robinson, Jim, 95
Robots, 179, 180
Robust strategies, role of
    futures-creative leaders in
    designing, 112–16
Rogers, Will, 149
Role model, leader as, 54,
    116–17

Scanning time, 128–29
Scott Paper, 136
Sears, Roebuck, 26
Security, through military
    power, 16–17
Self, management of, 50
Self-realization, happiness
    through, 17–23
Self-respect, 102
Shakespeare, William, 81
Shaw, George Bernard, 123
Shell Oil, 127
Sleaze factor, 112
Sloan, Alfred P., 6
Smucker, J. M., Company, 145
Southern California Edison
    Company (SCE), 138–40
Space sciences, 31
Spokesperson, futures-creative
    leader as, 76–77
Stakeholder intelligence
    systems, interest of futures-
    creative leaders in, 111

Stengel, Casey, 73
Strategies, role of futures-
    creative leaders in
    designing robust, 112–16
Strategy processes, 136–40
Superconductivity, 31, 181

Technological change, 42
Technological initiative, 179
Technological superiority,
    30–33
Telecommunications, 32
  combination of computers
    and, 32
Teleconferencing, 32
Teleshopping, 31
Teresa, Mother, 46
Terrorism, 16–17
Thinking, organizing for long-
    range, 158
3M, 179
Thriving on Chaos (Peters), 41
Tinker, Grant, 77–78
Tjosvold, Dean, 94
Trend monitoring, use of, by
    futures-creative leader,
    108–9, 110
Trends, failure of leaders to
    recognize important, 25–27
Trust
  developing, 118
  importance of, 101
  management of, 49–50
Two-income families, 20–21

Unemployment, 15, 19
United States
  basis for optimism for, 1–2,
    4, 189
  credit status of, 14–15
  decline of, as world power,
    17, 25–26
  family income in, 15, 20–21
  GNP in, 13–14
  imports/exports, 38, 39

net foreign liabilities of, 14
pessimism for future of, 1,
   2-3
productivity, 3, 14
unemployment in, 15, 19

Values
  ranking of, 102
  role of, in management of
    change, 64-65
Vickers, Sir Geoffrey, 65
Videocassette recorders, 180
Videotex, 179
Vision, development of, by
    futures-creative leader,
    105-7
Visionary leadership, 53
Voice messaging, 179

Wall Street Journal, 134
Warner Communications, 111
Washington, George, 192
Welles, Orson, 82
Westinghouse, George, 46
Work, role of, in self-
    realization, 18-19
World citizen, becoming,
    117-18

Xerox Corporation, 132-33